Y0-CCX-445

The Rhetoric of the British Peace Movement

Issues and Spokesmen Series

A RANDOM HOUSE STUDY IN SPEECH

GENERAL EDITOR   Don Geiger
University of California, Berkeley

 Random House, NEW YORK

THE
RHETORIC
of
THE
BRITISH
PEACE
MOVEMENT

◖ ◖ ◖

EDITED, WITH INTRODUCTIONS, BY

Charles W. Lomas
University of California, Los Angeles

Michael Taylor
San Francisco State College

Acknowledgments

◐ ◐ ◐

Grateful acknowledgment is made for permission to reprint the following works:

"Peace and War" from Donald Soper's *Tower Hill, 12:30* (London: Epworth Press, 1963), pp. 44–50. Reprinted by permission of the publishers, Epworth Press.

"No Defense Against Nuclear Attack," Sir Richard Acland's speech, from [Hansard] *Parliamentary Debates,* (Commons) 5th ser., 538 (1955): cols. 679–689. Reprinted by permission of Copyright Section, H. M. Stationery Office.

"Naked to the Conference Table," by Aneurin Bevan, from *Report of the Fifty-Sixth Annual Conference of the Labour Party* (London, 1957), pp. 179–183.

"Britain and the Nuclear Bomb," J. B. Priestley, from *New Statesman,* November 2, 1957, pp. 554–556. Reprinted by permission of *New Statesman.*

"Steps to Nuclear Disarmament," speech to the CND rally, February 18, 1958, by Lord Bertrand Russell. Reproduced by permission of Continuum 1, Limited, Lord Russell's literary agent, and McMaster University.

"Stand by Humanity," speech to the CND rally, February 18, 1958, by A. J. P. Taylor. Reconstructed from contemporary reports and approved by A. J. P. Taylor.

"Massive Retaliation Is Massive Nonsense," May 2, 1958, p. 5. Reprinted by permission of Tribune Publications, Limited.

"Debate at Scarborough," Frank Cousins and Hugh Gaitskells' speeches are presented in full from the *Report of the Fifty-Ninth Annual Conference of the Labour Party* (London, 1960), pp. 178–180, 195–201.

Preface

◖ ◗ ◖

The *Issues and Spokesmen Series* has been developed as a response to a need widely expressed in the areas of rhetoric and public address: in public speaking and written composition, in speech fundamentals, discussion, argumentation, and persuasion, and in rhetorical, political, and social criticism. Broadly, instructors and students of these matters desire an enriched rhetorical substance to complement the prevailing emphasis on method and general principles.

What is particularly needed, we agree in department meetings and at conventions, are more collections of speeches and writings focused on a significant theme or problem; or we search for concrete models of excellent persuasion and argument in connection with questions truly relevant to our students' increasingly active interest in "participatory" democracy; or we want materials that will encourage depth and range in critical analysis of particular problems, as we also wish for more studies designed to excite students to independent research; or we seek striking illustrations of the ways in which speakers and writers strive to effect politically and socially consequential attitudes and decisions. These are the kinds of material that the Random House series of books on *Issues and Spokesmen* will help to supply.

Certainly I do not suggest that these books will exhaust our educational need for speeches and writings that mean business in the realm of public affairs, or that they are our only available resources. My more sober aim, having identified the *Issues and Spokesmen* books as essays in provisioning rhetoric with appropriate substance, is to describe briefly the general design and pattern of this group of books.

The term "Issues" in the series title is best understood in the popular sense of "matter the decision of which is of special or public importance," and each book focuses on a significant controversy or question of public policy. Thus each volume contains a selection by its author-editor of speeches, or speeches and writings, by important spokesmen organized around an issue of major contemporary importance or importance to its time and clear relevance to our own. Each book also contains its author-editor's fairly long essay, covering all or some of such matters as the social, political, and intellectual environment of the issue; the background of the issue in history and rhetorical tradition; a description of the careers and roles of the spokesmen involved; or an account of the rhetorical techniques and the principles of analysis with which the student will be concerned as he becomes familiar with the issue and reexamines the speeches and writings. Speeches are presented chronologically and, wherever possible, in their entirety.

Headnotes and footnotes serve familiar functions—identifying speakers, the immediate occasion of a given speech, allusions requiring explanation, and the like. In addition, special interrogative footnotes draw the student more thoughtfully into the speech—its language, line of argument, and techniques. Questions and comments in these footnotes are not intended to preempt the student's own critical focus. Rather, they will serve as suggestive examples of what perceptive critics notice and question when analyzing a text. Broader implications of the speeches and writings are considered in each volume's sections for inquiry. The latter material serves as an inductive guide to students' further examination and discussion of a given issue.

Since my purpose is to comment generally, I shall say little about that which is nonetheless the most important aspect of the series, the individuality of the separate works. Each of these books bears the distinctive stamp of its author or coauthors; and each book represents an independent interest in substance and approach, as in toto the volumes reflect the common interests of expert students of the rhetoric of public affairs. I think that many other readers will share my admiration for the workmanship of the individual authors of these volumes and take pleasure in their educational contributions.

Don Geiger

Contents

◑ ◑ ◑

The Rhetoric of the British Peace Movement

One
◑ ◑ ◑
Introduction

THE RHETORIC OF PROTEST

A characteristic feature of organized society is that it seeks to perpetuate its institutions. Some members of such a society instinctively cling to the past—a past usually romanticized and distorted in memory. Some who once had been sensitive to the need for change and instrumental in bringing it about now may be convinced that the struggle for change that they won in their youth has so reformed society that new changes are unnecessary. The institutions that they established to formalize the change may have become ends in themselves. They therefore resist modification of those institutions, seeing it as an attack upon the reforms they once attained by supreme efforts. As Wendell Phillips puts it: "Parties and sects laden with the burden of securing their own success cannot afford to risk new ideas." [1] Because human institutions, like human beings, are imperfect, there is a need for continuous challenge to the status quo. The nature of that challenge depends upon the degree of rigidity

[1] Wendell Phillips, "*The Scholar in a Republic: Address at the Centennial Anniversary of the Phi Beta Kappa of Harvard College*" (Boston: Lee and Shepard, 1881), p. 21.

3

of society and the magnitude of the imperfections. It also depends on the degree of prophetic zeal possessed by those who seek change, and on the extent to which protesters stand to benefit from the modifications in the social order that they advocate.

In an open society, where free speech and press prevail, protest has usually taken the form of spoken or written agitation against the existing order. However, at times protesters have argued that words alone are not enough. No argument, they say, is possible when no one will listen. Like the Missouri mule, society must be hit over the head with a hammer to be forced to pay attention to the words that may follow. So it is that agitation, even in an open society, sometimes takes the activist forms of marches, sit-ins, disruptions of activities, and even violence. Although some who pursue these tactics may prefer them to more peaceful methods, for most participants, such actions are the result of frustration rather than of malice. They indulge in violence in the belief that words will be heard and negotiation attempted only when authorities see the possibility of losing the established order if communication is not established with dissidents.

In order to achieve their goals, however, protesters must eventually use written or spoken persuasion. Even if they should succeed in seizing and holding power by force, their ability to establish a new and stable order without repression would be dependent on winning the support of public opinion. For those who do not contemplate forceful revolution, the need for persuasion is even more obvious. Thus, the rhetoric of protest seeks to influence the beliefs of important segments of the public so that political pressure may be brought to bear upon legislators and administrators. Where economic interests or improvement of social conditions are at stake, the contest may be for the vote of a minority who will subordinate every issue to one, thus exercising the balance of power. Thus in mid-nineteenth-century Britain, the leaders of the Anti–Corn Law League subordinated every other issue to the repeal of the corn laws and forced British politicians to vote their will. In twentieth-century America, the Prohibition amendment was enacted through the pressure of the Anti–Saloon League minority exercising the balance of power between the Republican and Democratic parties. There are three steps to an agitation whose goal is seizure of power without force: (1) to win over a substantial body of public opinion to the views of the agitators, (2) to persuade important political units that acceptance of these views will result in their winning elections, (3) to convert this political support to political power.

The Campaign for Nuclear Disarmament (CND) in its initial stages from 1958 to 1961 was an example of such a grand strategy. It came close to succeeding, and in the process it left an imprint on world attitudes toward war that may yet produce positive results. Those hoped for by the founders were only partially attained, but an analysis of the methods used by the participants may cast some light on the importance of the issue as well as on the nature of the rhetoric of revolution.

To put the CND in perspective, however, it is necessary to review the background of a long series of protests against war.

HISTORICAL DEVELOPMENT OF PEACE MOVEMENTS

From the earliest records of human history to the present, there have been few periods when wars have not been fought. Paralleling man's efforts at self-extermination have been other, not as well publicized, attempts to establish peace. These peace plans for the most part have emanated from centers of power, having their origins and focuses now in kings, popes, and religious bodies; now in mercantile interests, nationalism, and imperialism; now in public opinion and political organizations. One of the first efforts at peace by governmental action was the Delphic Amphictyonic Council, the cooperative effort of ancient Greek city-states to protect the sacred places and to call a sacred truce in order that the Olympic games might be conducted at periodic intervals. Another pattern of peace attempts can be found in the Pax Romana, Pax Brittania, and Pax Americana. These were times of enforced peace maintained by continual battles on besieged frontiers while the illusion of peace at home was preserved by superior military strength.

Within modern times, federations and alliances have sought to bring about conditional kinds of peace. The ends of these coalitions were variously to preserve the status quo, to give breathing space for recovery from previous wars, or to separate friend from foe and enable participating members to focus their combined efforts against the enemy. Although loose federations of European sovereigns have appeared periodically since the Crusades, the Napoleonic wars brought about a series of nineteenth-century efforts to organize groupings of national states. A Holy Alliance sponsored by the czar of Russia was followed by a Quadruple Alliance of Great Britain, Russia, Prussia, and Austria. The ensuing Concert of Europe was brief and ineffective. In 1884 James Lorimer of Edinburgh proposed, in *The Institutes of the Law of Nations,* an international government with an executive exclusively separate and international. Multilateral disarmament, proportionally arranged to maintain the status quo, was one prominent feature of this proposal.

This plan, however, was somewhat eclipsed by a massive peace effort launched by Russia. Czar Nicholas II issued a call in 1898 to the nations of Europe to send representatives to the Hague to promote international understanding and peace. Although all twenty-six nations invited attended, disarmament proposals did not get far. Among the topics discussed were pacific settlement of international conflict and rules for land and maritime warfare. A Permanent Court of Arbitration, which eventually handled fifteen cases, was established.

A second Hague meeting in 1907, this time with forty-four states represented, firmed up the proposals of the first conference: obligatory arbitration, a court of arbitral justice, and provision for a third conference in eight years.

This giant step toward world peace was strongly checked

when on June 28, 1914, the Archduke Francis Ferdinand, heir to the throne of Austria-Hungary was assassinated. The Great War (1914–1918) dwarfed all other previous conflicts —it involved the principal nations of the world and cost some 200 billion dollars and 8 million lives.

In the twentieth century the most ambitious organized effort at peaceful settlements, the League of Nations, eventually collapsed because of internal weaknesses: bickering among member nations, suspicion, lack of authority, inability to implement its decisions, lack of flexibility, and selective representation. At present writing the ultimate fate of the successor to the League, the United Nations, is at best uncertain. To many, it seems doubtful that governments will ever find a solution to the problems of war.

Simultaneous with nineteenth-century high-level governmental moves to gain national advantages under the guise of seeking peace, a new concept appeared—that peace could be secured only when public opinion could be so organized that rulers would hesitate to make war lest their own people might not follow them. At the heart of this new viewpoint was a group of Quaker reformers united in an organization that sought to propagandize the establishment of peace to the people of England. Led by William Allen, The Society for the Promotion of Permanent and Universal Peace had as its basic tenet, "war is inconsistent with the spirit of Christianity and the true interests of mankind." [2] The best means to maintain permanent and universal peace was upon the basis of Christian principles. During the course of its life, which extended up to the period of the Crimean War, the society, popularly known as the London Peace Society, was principally supported by Quakers. James Andrews recognizes three distinct phases in the society. The first phase, the religious phase (1816–1848), focused propaganda efforts on the distribution of religious tracts: closely worded

[2] The bulk of the information about the London Peace Society is drawn from an article by James Andrews, "Piety and Pragmatism: Rhetorical Aspects of the Early British Peace Movements," *Speech Monographs*, 34 (November 1967), 423–437.

documents of fifty to sixty pages in length. There were three basic goals of the society during this phase: to disseminate information that would educate and sway public opinion; to formulate a coherent creed or code of behavior; and to get people to act in accordance with such a code. In the first thirty years of the society's existence, 1,200,000 pieces of literature were distributed to subscribers, booksellers, judges, cabinet ministers, libraries, and members of the diplomatic service. Tracts were also translated and spread throughout Europe. In addition to these outlets, paid agents of the society traveled about England, distributing literature and addressing church groups. Gains were negligible; appeals to reform were geared to the pious intellectual; no real plan was offered except for each individual to renounce war.

The year 1848 ushered in the second and third phases of the society, phases that overlapped and operated simultaneously. The second, or pragmatic, phase began when Henry Richard, a Methodist minister active in social causes, became secretary. Together with Joseph Sturge, a Quaker who spread the cause in Birmingham, Richard represented a new activism. The target of the society's propaganda moved from the individual to government. Borrowing a device from the Chartists, the society circulated peace petitions, but never with very wide support. Lobbying occasionally produced better results, as in the case of the Paris Congress of 1856, where the collective efforts of Henry Richard, Joseph Sturge and Charles Hindley, the latter a Member of Parliament from Ashton, persuaded the delegates to insert an arbitration clause in the treaty. Another device was the Peace Congress, the first of which was held in London in 1843. The purposes of these international congresses were to draw attention to the peace movement and to generate international cooperation. A systematic program for pacifism gradually emerged, and the congresses took on an air of importance as men of reputation and influence participated in them.

The third, or political, phase began when two members of

Parliament, operating outside the context of the society, gave considerable impetus to the cause of peace. Richard Cobden, a political economist and advocate of free trade, and his political ally John Bright, also an economist, made pacifism a viable political doctrine. Moving away from the rather vague ideology of peace based on Christian principles, these two men developed a specific plan to prevent war by reduction of armaments, nonintervention in foreign affairs, and the use of arbitration to settle controversy.

Instead of arguing that any form of violence was morally wrong, Cobden and Bright maintained that aggressive foreign policies were disadvantageous to British interests in trade and international relations. Although they repeatedly dissociated themselves from the society's doctrine of nonresistance, both men kept in close touch with the leadership and addressed the peace congresses. Buffeted by the surge of British imperialism and scattered by the Crimean War issue, the London Peace Society clearly suffered from the basic dilemma of pacifism: "in peace time pacifism seems irrelevant—in war pacifism seems unpatriotic." [3]

The passage of the Military Service Act in January 1916 introduced universal conscription into Britain for the first time in its history and gave a new cause to the advocates of peace. Volunteers and professionals had filled the ranks prior to this period, but the need for the total mobilization of the nation no longer permitted this system to operate. All able-bodied citizens were subject to the draft regardless of personal convictions.[4] Organized pacifist activities, which grew out of the passage of the universal conscription act, were spearheaded by the Society of Friends, as pacifism had always been a fundamental tenet of their membership. The Quaker-led No Conscription Fellowship attacked the act directly, vowing to refuse to bear arms and opposing compulsory military service in Britain. The government re-

---

[3] *Ibid.*, p. 436.
[4] George Thayer, *The British Political Fringe* (London: Anthony Blond, Ltd., 1965), p. 156.

taliated with jail sentences and heavy fines. By the end of the
first year of the act's enforcement over 6,000 pacifists, Quaker
or otherwise, had been jailed for refusing to obey it.

The idea of the irrelevance of pacifism in peacetime once
more asserted itself during the period between the wars.
Pacifist activities were sporadic and lacked organization.
The No Conscription Fellowship was rechristened the No
More War Movement and continued pacifist activities.
Fenner Brockway, a founder of the fellowship, was turning
his efforts toward the future War Resisters International.
Other small pacifist organizations were also operating, but
independently of each other.

The Peace Pledge Union (PPU), founded in 1936, which
published *Peace News,* was the largest prewar pacifist organization. The membership of the PPU came largely from
the No More War Movement and the War Resisters International. By 1939 the PPU membership had grown to 130,-
000 Englishmen, all pledging not to support a war on
Britain's behalf. Of these, 51,000 declared themselves con-
scientious objectors who would not fight anyone at any time.
Although many held firm to their beliefs, the PPU was
decimated by the desertion of many who found Hitlerism
more terrible than war. Not until the war had ended was a
new pacifism possible.

On a Monday morning, the sixth of August, 1945, a single
bomb was dropped from a high altitude. The bomb measured only 28 inches by 120 inches, and it floated slowly
down attached to a parachute. At 2,200 feet it exploded over
the seaport city of Hiroshima, in southwest Japan on Hon-
shu Island. Like a latter-day Krakatoa, this bomb and the
one that fell on Nagasaki on August 9, 1945, had repercus-
sions of tremendous significance, ushering in a totally new
concept of warfare and mobilizing extensive efforts for disarmament and peace.

The sudden end of the war left peace groups puzzled and
disorganized. But by 1950 there appeared to be a coalescing
of antiwar supporters into four general categories that eventually formed the base for the Campaign for Nuclear Dis-

armament. First, there were those who adhered to the Quaker philosophy based on the Gospel's admonition that war is contrary to Christian principles. Second, there were those influenced by the teachings of Mahatma Gandhi, Indian leader and social reformer, whose philosophy of non-violent resistance had been successful in India. Third, there were the pacifists who supported civil disobedience if there was sufficient moral justification for it. And fourth, there was a general movement guided by Christians not restricted to the Society of Friends.

From 1950 to 1958 pacifist activities increased considerably. Operation Gandhi grew out of the Peace Pledge Union's Non-Violence Commission. Its objectives included: the cessation of the manufacture of atomic weapons, withdrawal of American forces from England, withdrawal of Britain from NATO, and the disbanding of all British armed forces. The PPU backed up its protests by demonstrations and sit-downs at military bases and defense research sites.

A basic weakness of the pacifist movement up to this time had been the lack of a broad-based, cooperative effort on the part of the small pacifist organizations. This was to be a major consideration in the formation of the CND.

A CRITICAL FRAMEWORK FOR THE STUDY OF SPEECHES

The ostensible purpose of agitation in Great Britain against nuclear armaments was to solidify public opinion (or a substantial segment of it) in overt opposition to the development, manufacture, or use of nuclear explosives as a military weapon or as a diplomatic threat. The forces that coalesced in the Campaign for Nuclear Disarmament in 1958 had little in common except their determination to "ban the bomb." Some of them represented the pacifist elements, both religious and secular, which had been active in Britain for generations. The Peace Pledge Union, the No Conscription Fellowship (taken over between the wars and renamed the No More War Movement), and oldest of all, the Society of Friends, were typical pacifist organizations of long standing. On the other hand, some leaders of the new movement were intellectuals without previous association with peace movements, such as J. B. Priestley and A. J. P. Taylor. Some were Christian leaders who were horrified at the destructive power of nuclear war, even though they stopped short of complete pacifism, such as Canon L. J. Collins. The movement included politicians (mostly, but not exclusively, of the Labour party) and anarchists who had no faith in political parties, but preferred direct action against established institutions. It also included a multitude of ordinary people, dominantly but not exclusively young, who had never before participated actively in any political or social movement.

The speeches and essays in this book may be regarded as rhetorical efforts to mobilize these diverse forces and direct them toward the aim of abolishing nuclear warfare; to divert the course of the agitation so as to serve the special interests of one of the groups involved; or to channel energies toward modified goals, which might be easier to attain. In some cases the rhetoric seems to be directed at all the factions. In others the speaker or writer appears to be limiting his goal to influencing only a part of the potential audience. Because the nature of the speaker, his purpose, and his audience varies among these speeches, we will attempt in each case to identify these factors in such a way that the reader may make judgments about the nature of the controversy and the quality of the rhetoric advanced by the advocates.

In general the speakers had three main goals: (1) creation of strong hostility toward all forms of nuclear warfare, (2) creation of a desire to take an active part in ending all aspects of nuclear war including preparation for it, (3) winning support for specific programs to channel that desire into action. Some speakers, depending on their own abilities and on the nature of the audience and occasion, attempted only one or two of these. Some tried to achieve all three. In attempting to attain the first two, speakers and writers could easily create a high degree of identification with their audiences. The known facts and presumptions about the destructive power of the H-bomb appeared in government documents and in the speeches of cabinet ministers determined to maintain Britain's nuclear strike force. These facts were so terrible that speakers had little difficulty rousing their audiences to moral and even physical revulsion against the bomb. Thus Donald Soper could ask a Hyde Park questioner who supported the bomb: "Would you put a baby on the fire?" and after the heckler's denial, Soper could extend the image a thousandfold by graphically describing the effect of the bomb.[5]

Moreover it was not difficult for each member of the audience to identify his own well-being with the cause. It was easy to imagine that he himself might be incinerated or subjected to slow and painful radiation poisoning. He could easily picture his home and neighborhood destroyed, his city devastated, indeed his whole civilization terminated in an instant. He did not even need to fear being branded as a coward, for it is a natural human reaction to be afraid of the total destruction of oneself, one's friends, and one's society. Insofar as speeches and essays dealt with the first two goals, therefore, persuasion was relatively easy and unification of audiences attainable.

As to the third goal, however, there was no such unanimity. Even among those determined to end use of the bomb, there were acrimonious differences as to tactics. Some sought to use direct action: picketing, sit-downs, disruption of public services. Some sought to demonstrate to political leaders the strength of the movement by mass rallies, marches, and petitions. Some sought to gain control of the means of political action. The realities of British politics meant that they thus should have concentrated on capturing the Labour party, an end very nearly attained in 1960. But even if a majority could have been mustered against the bomb, there was not unanimity as to the means of its abolition. Some

5 Personal observation, May, 1961.

concentrated primarily on banishing tests; some sought action only by diplomatic means; some favored unilateral action by Britain alone; some directed their attacks against the American alliance; some expressed hostility to nuclear activities anywhere in the world. As in most radical alliances, it was much easier to agree on the nature of the problem than to unite on a program of action or the means by which it should be implemented.

If we are to examine the rhetoric of a complex agitation such as the Ban-the-Bomb movement, Kenneth Burke's description of the key rhetorical concept of "identification" is of value. Although the idea is not originally Burke's, his use of the term suggests new insights and applications, some of which may be helpful here. Burke defines identification as "consubstantiality," an almost mystical term borrowed from the language of philosophical theology. "A doctrine of *consubstantiality* either explicit or implicit may be necessary to any way of life. For substance in the old philosophies was an *act;* and a way of life is an *acting-together,* and in acting together, men have common sensations, concepts, images, ideas, attitudes that make them consubstantial." [6] In the rhetoric of the CND, speakers and writers sought to bring about identification of disparate groups with each other, to cause them to identify with their leaders, and then to "act together" in a common purpose. In such symbolic acts as mass rallies in Trafalgar Square; Easter marches to or from the Aldermaston atomic energy plants; wearing the drooping cross, symbol of the CND; or uniting in public condemnations of H-bomb tests, a high degree of identification was attained. In more controversial matters dealing with actions to be taken, the differences were accentuated and identification could not be reached either within the group or between the group and its leaders.

In studying these examples of H-bomb rhetoric, therefore, certain questions may be asked:

1. What was the speaker's purpose? to demonstrate the

[6] Kenneth Burke, *A Rhetoric of Motives* (New York: George Braziller, Inc., 1950), p. 21.

moral repulsiveness of nuclear warfare? to create a desire to act against nuclear warfare? to win support for a program of action against nuclear warfare? Given the audience and the nature of the occasion, was this the best purpose to adopt? Could more have been achieved by a different purpose?

2. To what extent did the speaker succeed in identifying himself and his purpose with his audience? Did he understand their needs and aspirations? What means were open to him to achieve identification? What barriers existed? Did his rhetoric help his hearers to believe that he shared their values? Did his rhetoric help to surmount the barriers? In what way might he have used values differently? Would the change have been an improvement?

3. If identification was achieved, did the speaker move the audience beyond the point of agreement indicated by their attendance? In doing so, did he maintain identification or did he alienate all or part of the group?

4. What were his methods of gaining and using identification? an attempt to get the audience to trust his judgment? argument based on moral or religious principles? argument based on practical considerations? use of emotionally loaded descriptions, exaggeration, and verbal tricks? To what extent did any of these appear to aid in identifying members of the audience with each other and with the speaker? To what extent did they appear to aid the speaker in accomplishing his purpose?

Two

● ● ●

Prelude to the Campaign for Nuclear Disarmament

The period after 1945 in Britain was a curious mixture of dying imperialist sentiment and militant pacifism. Thus Winston Churchill could declare with the approval of a large minority of the British electorate in 1945 that he "did not become the King's first minister to preside over the liquidation of the British Empire." Large and enthusiastic crowds turned out for the jingoist military shows known as "tattoos," and in the fifties, to counter growing pacifist sentiment, a proimperialism group gained strength under the name of the League of Empire Loyalists.

At the same time, however, pacifist sentiment, always latently strong even in the nineteenth century, was beginning to polarize around the antinuclear theme. The reaction against the horrors of nuclear warfare was evident from the beginning of the atomic age. In August of 1945, for example, the dean of St. Albans refused to allow the cathedral to be used for a V-J Day celebration, in protest against the Hiroshima and Nagasaki bombings. In the years that passed there were scattered protests, blunted by lack of knowledge created by a veil of secrecy around atomic research. In 1947 Kingsley Martin argued in the *New Statesman* for atomic neutrality as the only possible defense for "these vulnerable islands." In 1948 pacifists were concentrating on conscription as an issue; yet at least one major antinuclear meeting was held in which Ritchie Calder (later to be vice-chairman of CND) was one of the participants.[1] During the same period pacifist members of Parliament were protesting against Prime Minister Attlee's decision to manufacture atomic bombs. By 1951 the British Non-Violence Commission was making plans for "Operation Gandhi," proposing an end to the American alliance and NATO and proposing also complete British disarmament. Throughout the fifties there were many isolated protests in Parliament and out, but there was no concerted effort to direct all the protesting groups into a common channel.

Peace and War

DONALD SOPER

To examine the pattern of the pre-CND protests, we have selected two examples of the rhetoric of this era. One of these was published five years after the organization of CND, but it is a reconstruction of the speaker's standard approach to the issue of peace over many years.

The Rev. Dr. Donald Soper (now Lord Soper) is a Methodist minister with the title of Superintendent of the West London Mission, a complex of church and social agencies centered at Kingsway Hall in London's West End. Dr. Soper, however, has been appearing in the role of social agitator for more than forty years every Wednesday noon on Tower Hill, and for more than thirty years on Sundays in Hyde Park, speaking about his view of the relevance of

[1] Christopher Driver, *The Disarmers* (London: Hodder and Stoughton, Ltd., 1964), p. 18.

*Christianity to the social conflicts of the age.[2] His primary
themes are Christian socialism and Christian pacifism. Because he has been an unqualified pacifist throughout his long
career, he has rejected the most militant aspects of CND
while embracing its philosophical base. His opposition to
violence in any form is well reflected in his reconstruction of
a Tower Hill dialogue on the issue of peace and war. The
dialogue is both dated and timeless. Since Dr. Soper always
relates his discussions to the questions of his audience, they
deal with immediate issues. Since these issues are merely
variations on a timeless problem, they are never out of date.
There are only a few references in the dialogue to events of
the 1960s. What he was saying in 1963, he had been saying in
various forms for forty years. For this reason, this selection is
an excellent example of the antiwar rhetoric of the committed pacifists who prepared the groundwork for the new
breed of antinuclear agitators who emerged in the CND.*

In this chapter I want to speak about the many questions
that are continually being asked on Tower Hill in relation
to peace and war.

Looking back over thirty-five years, I cannot remember a
single meeting at which this problem has not been raised. In
the mind of the man in the street, so far as I have met him,
war is his greatest anxiety and peace his most vital concern.

I would like you to imagine that you are on Tower Hill,
somewhere near the back of the crowd, and I will try to give
you an idea of the questions as they arise and the answers
that I have attempted to make. I want to make two things
clear at the outset. These are actual questions that have
been, and are still being, asked; and the answers are the
ones that I personally have been, and still am, giving. You
may think of better questions, you may agree or disagree
with these answers, but this will be a faithful record of what
actually happens on the Hill. You may feel that some of

[2] For a longer analysis of Soper's rhetoric, see Charles W. Lomas, "Agitator in a Cassock," *Western Speech*, 27 (Winter 1963), 16–24.

what I say is far-fetched, but at least I have fetched it myself. As you stand in the crowd you will not be able to see most of the questioners, so I shall not trouble to describe them. If I simply state the question and then give the answer, the procedure will not be much different from that of the actual meeting. So here goes.

'You say you are a Christian and out for peace. How do you explain the fact that after 2,000 years of Christianity we had the worst war in history?'

But have we had 2,000 years of Christianity? Surely Chesterton is right when he says: 'Christianity has not been tried and found wanting—it's been found difficult and left untried.'

'But hasn't the Church waged merciless wars in the name of Jesus Christ? Did not the Crusaders wear a cross on their shirt-fronts? Don't bishops bless aircraft-carriers? In the war, didn't all sides call upon God to help them?'

That is true. No Christian who thinks about these things at all is in any doubt as to the terrible failures of Christ's Church. As a parson, I always feel that I could put the case against the Church much better than you do. But what you are condemning is the Christian, not his Lord.

'We judge Christianity as we find it.'

Undoubtedly; but have you found it? Surely the Church is more than an institution; it is a living fellowship, and you can never judge a fellowship from the outside. A man is always better than his actions. You wouldn't be content to be judged merely by what you have done or failed to do. You would say to your critic: 'Yes, but you don't understand my difficulties and my temptations.' The same is true of the Church. Believe me, I am ready and willing to admit every accusation that you can bring; but that's not the whole story. I can understand your bitterness—I wonder whether you have ever tried to understand our penitence. There is a true spirit of peace in the Church today.

'That's all eyewash! The Church today is the same as it always was.'

Now, of course, you are talking out of your hat. Have you been to a church lately?

'No; and I don't intend to go, either.'

Very good; but you mustn't assume that you can get a true picture of Christianity from the daily newspapers. How many peace societies do you think there are at work in the various denominations? There are at least five Christian societies whose representatives meet from many nations, which are striving their utmost to promote peace. Where do you think the United Nations would be without the support it receives from organized Christianity? Why, I belong to a Peace Fellowship of over 600 ministers in the Methodist Church, pledged absolutely to renounce war.

'We don't trust you. I lay you were a recruiting officer in the last war, and you'd do it again.'[3]

You are quite sure about that?

'Dead certain.'

How old do you think I am?

'Old enough to know better.'

Precisely—I do know better. When the First World War broke out I had reached the age of eleven, and at fifteen I was a bayonet-fighting instructor in a cadet corps, teaching other boys how to do No. 1 butt stroke. Like thousands of my own generation, I had to reconcile bayonet-fighting with the Christianity I was slowly coming to understand, and I found it couldn't be done.

'Then are we to understand that as a Christian you won't take part in another war?'

I will not. I know that war is absolutely contrary to the spirit and teaching of Jesus Christ.

'That all sounds very simple, but what do you mean by renouncing war? How can you logically do that when you and everybody else are tied up in a world of violence?'

I know; and I have long since given up the questionable

[3] Soper does not say so, but he made pacifist speeches regularly throughout World War II. Knowing this, how would you evaluate his personal references, here and later in the speech?

ideal of trying to be logical. We do live in a world of war, and we simply can't escape all its implications. If I were logical, I should have to refuse to eat food which came to me by methods of violence; and that would not leave me a very varied diet. I suppose I should have to make my own clothes; even then I don't know where I should get the cloth from. War and nationalism and the economic system are all mixed up together, and whatever we do we can't renounce everything that belongs to violence. However, you won't make me believe that we can't break into that vicious circle at some point. Why not at the point of war? To make up our minds that we will follow the Christian way to peace would release new forces in this world of ours, and help us to build the Kingdom of Peace in every sphere.

'Oh! So you do believe in force?'

Of course I do. If my little granddaughter is in danger of falling into the fire, I pick her up and carry her out of danger. That is force, but it is creative force. It saves, it doesn't destroy.

'That's all very well; but what would happen if a burglar came into your bedroom and began to knock your wife about—what would you do then?'

There are several answers to that. First of all, you don't know my wife. In the second place, you don't know much about burglars; and, in the third place, I am certain that if I took up the Christian attitude as I think it to be, and did not try to knock his head off, he would not knock my wife about. You think that's all rot, eh? Well! I shall stick to that faith, and if this highly improbable occasion does arise, I intend to test it out. I'll bring the burglar up to Tower Hill the week after as a witness! After all, I've had a bit of experience of this sort of thing. I have been knocked off this wall in my time, and the situation had all the earmarks of a first-class row; I took the attitude I've just been describing and it worked. Again, some of you may remember 'Tiger Face'. He threatened and fully intended to knife me, but he didn't; and it was his knowledge that I wouldn't fight that stopped him. You see, refusing to be violent is not becoming a doormat. It is allowing what I believe to be the power of God to flow through you. The Iron and Bamboo Curtains are not the same barriers after you have faced them in the Spirit of Christ. For that reason I don't believe that there are any circumstances or situations in which, of necessity, violence is indispensable and reason inoperative. We may be called to take up our cross and give our lives for that Christian truth. We shan't be taking other people's or throwing our own away.

Let's get back to the larger issue. How can I stand by and watch a foreign army invade my country, burn my home and attack my children? Apart from the question whether they would, if we were Christians, and they might, what lies behind your question? You believe war is justified in order to defend your hearth and home. You would have some sort of case if you really could stand at your front door and defend your loved ones. The plain fact is that the bomber aeroplane and now the nuclear weapon have made the 'defence argument' quite futile.

If a war came, what would happen? In the nuclear age the first answer is, of course, that we do not know, but this ignorance is only of detail; the overall pattern is all too terribly obvious. There might be some sort of waiting period in which both sides would hesitate to use their ultimate weapons, but the moment those weapons were used the results would be catastrophic for everybody, young and old, the trained and the defenceless, soldiers and civilians. Mutual, indiscriminate, universal destruction would mark the course of this supreme insanity, and 'defence' would be absolutely out of the question. The only consolation for you would be that probably at the same time as you and your defenceless wife and children were being killed, the wives and children and those men opposite you would be suffering a similar fate.

At this point, gentle reader, Mr James Wilson, of 12 Beanbody Buildings, asks a question. He has been standing quite close to you—in fact, you may well be Mr. Wilson yourself.

'Mr Speaker, I agree with a certain amount of what you say. I can't go all the way with you, but my problem is not what I won't do, but what I will do. Can't Christians, and non-Christians for that matter, get together and form a united front? Even if we differ about a number of these ultimate things, is that any reason why we shouldn't work together on some agreed programme?'

No reason at all. The hope of peace is to meet the united forces of war which are held together by fear and greed, with the army of peace, disciplined, organized and welded into a great fellowship of love and sacrifice. With all its imperfection the United Nations is the hope of the world, and that U.N. is your opportunity and mine, here and now. Let us stop talking about 'it' and begin to talk about 'we'. The channel through which you can be of service is the United Nations. Join up and support it.

The manufacture and use of nuclear power in bombs and guided missiles has entirely transformed the world picture of mass violence and power politics. If you can't go the whole hog, as I do as a pacifist, then you can, and I believe you should, join in the campaign for the banning of nuclear weapons lock, stock, and barrel. Everybody recognizes that if they were once used nothing but a shambles would be left. Every responsible statesman agrees that there ought to be a multilateral repudiation of them. What you and I can do is to press for a gesture to be made. I believe that this country could make it. I cannot foretell or even forecast what would be the result, but it is my strong conviction that such unilateral action would break the vicious circle.

'If you're talking about unilateral disarmament, why don't you support the civil disobedience campaigns by joining in the sit-downs in Whitehall and Trafalgar Square? The Suffragettes succeeded in making their point, didn't they?' [4]

4 In the pre-CND period, Soper did in fact participate in some nonviolent direct action. By 1961, however, he had become disillusioned with some of the violent actions accompanying demonstrations and adopted the position stated here. Do you agree with his change of attitude?

What I will not accept, and have never accepted, is the idea that by civil disobedience you can coerce people into taking an attitude which by reason or conviction they would not be prepared to take. We have a democratic opportunity of reversing the Government's programme, and we ought to use it to the full, because if once we threw it away we should be inviting others to throw it away as well. The whole point about the Suffragettes is that they hadn't the vote and therefore had no free opportunity of expressing what they wanted. I believe we should use the democratic weapon until it is exhausted, and not turn to another one which by its use will enfeeble and, I think, ultimately disable the democratic weapon altogether.[5]

I have a great deal of sympathy for the people who sit down in Trafalgar Square. What I have not is a mind to go with it, and therefore I'm putting my own case as a pacifist. If you are concerned to secure the abolition of violence, then you must be very careful that you don't so extend this kind of propaganda as to put off people who might be convinced by other means. I think that is a very important point. What I want to get out of people's minds is the idea that, because a man is prepared to undergo the indignity of arrest and imprisonment for what he does, that confers a cachet on the argument, because it does nothing of the sort.

Don't think that I am in any way aspersing these people. I'm only saying you've got to make your choice, and that pretty clearly. I cannot accept this as the right way for a pacifist. I can see that it is the right way for an agitator, who has the very strongest conviction and believes that this is a preferable form of propaganda. But, unless you can finally convince the other man, you haven't won him; and, whatever else you do, if you are against violence, any form of coercion which, by its application or by its implications, will invite coercion on the other side is a questionable weapon to use.

[5] Soper has long been an active participant in Labour party politics, believing that the party would ultimately embrace the unilateral disarmament position.

After all, what is the only available method of ultimately changing the programme of the present Government? It is the persuasion that we make whereby enough people vote the other way. I can't think of any other save the Communist one, and I reject it. The Communist answer is simple and very realistic. You organize yourselves so that you can by violent means if necessary—and they will be violent means—overthrow the Government which will never give way to persuasion and will never be reconciled to another point of view.

'I think that's more rational.'

I don't. I think it is completely irrational, because what happens in the end is that, instead of getting rid of the violence, you double it. If you reject violence, you've got to take up the cross, if you like, of gradualism, or at least you've got to take up the cross of personal conviction.

Perhaps the appropriate thing I can say at this point is that if ordinary people believed that they must have a hand in this work, and conscientiously supported its every move that was made towards genuine peacemaking, they would create a dynamic force which ultimately would be irresistible, because it is God's Will.

QUESTIONS AND REFERENCES

1. If you were a member of Soper's Tower Hill or Hyde Park audience, what questions would you ask him? Can you predict his probable answers?

2. How might you apply Soper's argument about civil disobedience and the democratic process to the actions of contemporary American protest groups? Discuss the validity of his point of view.

3. Most textbooks on public speaking emphasize the concept of feedback from an audience, which in turn influences the way in which the speaker develops his ideas. With Soper's audience, the feedback is explicit. Try removing the audience questions from the text. How would the speaker deal with the same ideas if he could not play off specific audience responses?

4. In addition to the references cited, you might like to consult Heathcote Williams, *The Speakers* (New York: Grove Press, 1964), and

Donald Soper, *Advocacy of the Gospel* (New York: Abingdon Press, 1961). The former is a light-hearted discussion of Hyde Park oratory; the latter is Soper's own explanation of his purpose in preaching—particularly, preaching at Tower Hill and Hyde Park.

No Defence Against Nuclear Attack

SIR RICHARD ACLAND

A dedicated but small group of Labour members of Parliament had maintained a pacifist position since World War I. Fenner Brockway had been a leader of the No Conscription Fellowship since its inception during World War I. Ramsay Macdonald and George Lansbury, who had been among the leaders of the Labour party in the years after the war, were both pacifists. After 1945 it was Labour Prime Minister Clement Attlee who made the decision to accept nuclear armaments, but strong opposition began to be expressed within the party. Among the new leaders, the degree of opposition varied from the moderate position of Richard Crossman to the vacillation of Aneurin Bevan to the militant stands of Sidney Silverman, Harold Davies, Emrys Hughes, and Michael Foot. Yet within the parliamentary party,[6] those opposed to any use of nuclear armaments remained a distinct although highly articulate minority.

Perhaps the most significant political action leading up to the Campaign for Nuclear Disarmament was the dramatic conversion of Sir Richard Acland to the antinuclear-warfare cause. This conversion culminated in his House of Commons speech of March 10, 1955, reproduced here. A deeply religious man, Sir Richard had never been able to find a political party through which he could express his deepest convictions. In 1941 he had left the Liberal party to become the leader of an independent party, the moderately socialist Commonwealth party. This party failed to win a following,

[6] The term is used in England to refer to members of a political party who hold seats in parliament.

so he joined the Labour party in 1947, becoming the Labour member of Parliament for Gravesend. In this community he operated from an all-party base, appealing to the Establishment through his Anglican orthodoxy and to the workers through his socialist beliefs.[7]

By 1955 Sir Richard had reached the conclusion that he could no longer accept the position either of his own party or of the Conservatives on the issue of nuclear bombs. He resigned his seat in Parliament and declared his intention of taking his position to the electorate of Gravesend for vindication. Unfortunately, the dissolution of Parliament and the calling of a general election prevented him from fighting a one-issue campaign. The vote of the Labour electors was split between Acland and the official Labour candidate that ran against him, and a Conservative, Peter Kirk, claimed the seat for the next nine years. Acland retired from politics, although not from antinuclear efforts. His speech is credited with giving new impetus to the H-bomb opponents and stimulating the growth of movements that culminated in the CND.

Although Acland follows the parliamentary convention of relating his remarks to those of the speaker who preceded him, it is evident that he is striking out on a very different and more significant issue than those in the speeches preceding his.

I regret that I cannot follow the hon. and gallant Member for Macclesfield (Air Commodore Harvey) in his arguments on many of the detailed points on which he has made such very constructive suggestions, beyond saying that I was interested in the point he made about the possibility of fog grounding the whole of our fighter force. That only goes to emphasise a point which is part of the foundation of my

7 In 1964 a number of prominent Gravesend Conservatives expressed to me their deep respect for Acland, "an educated man and a gentleman," in contrast to the successful Labour party candidate of that year, an able, self-educated man whose working-class origins were obvious in his speech and manner. C. W. L.

own view, namely, that there is, of course, no defence against thermo-nuclear attack.

Although the hon. and gallant Member urged that to remedy the possibility of our finding ourselves with fog-bound piloted fighters we should go ahead as fast as possible in the construction of the guided missile. I think that he would agree that we are not likely to perfect the guided anti-aircraft missile before our potential opponents have perfected the guided ground-to-ground, aggressive, long-range rocket, with a thermo-nuclear warhead, against which the guided counter rocket is no defence whatever.[8]

In any event, I want to leave these relatively small considerations, because this evening it is my purpose to oppose the Air Estimates on the grounds that they make provision for the strategic bomber force whose sole purpose is to carry the hydrogen bomb. I believe that that decision is wrong. I do not regard it as being relatively wrong or wrong in some small way. I regard it as being absolutely wrong, and I believe that the taking of this decision is the crucial decision which heads us towards disaster: whereas, if we had the courage, the vision and the clearsightedness to refrain from this decision, the defence of our country and the peace of the world for the next quarter or half century might yet be secured.

I feel so intensely on this problem that I have to make a personal point. It is no longer possible for me—or rather to be more accurate I should say that for rather special reasons it is only possible for me for a few days longer—to go along with the majority of my colleagues on these benches who take the other view. This, therefore, is certainly the last speech that I shall make in this House except on the other side of the next Gravesend by-election, and it could, therefore, be the last speech that I shall make here for a quite considerable time. I have to face that possibility.[9]

---

[8] You might wish to compare this controversy with the 1969 debate in the United States Congress over deployment of the antiballistic missile system.

[9] Acland is referring to his decision to resign and seek approval of his

I want to make another personal point, with your permission, Sir, and that of the House. In taking the line which I take this evening, with this emphasis, I am bound to start with the word *Peccavi*.[10] I have myself sinned in regard to this issue because, of course, I should have protested, or protested much more vigorously, not merely against the hydrogen bomb today but against the A-bomb and the strategic bomber force in each year that this matter has come forward since the war.

I did, indeed, make a speech at this time last year against the strategic bomber force, and, to that limited extent, I am consistent. For the rest, I can only say two things in extenuation of my failure. One is that in the last 12 months something has happened. The hydrogen bomb has been actually exploded, and Japanese fishermen have been killed hundreds of miles from the explosion.[11] That is something which affects anyone's emotions, and makes one understand and grasp the significance of things which, to be quite candid, one ought to have grasped before but did not. There is another change in the situation that has occurred during the last 12 months which I shall come to in the course of what I shall have to say.

Now, in considering the strategic bomber force, with all its terrible implications to humanity, I am bound to say, first of all, that the purely pacifist argument is enormously strong. When honestly stated that argument is quite simple. It is that this sort of thing is morally wrong. There is no room whatever for calculation about any consequences in the pacifist argument. Whatever the consequences may be, they assert that war is wrong.

---

stand on nuclear weapons through the medium of a by-election. How would an American congressman handle a similar issue?

10 Sir Richard's use of the liturgical term meaning "I have sinned" is a reflection of his deep personal religious commitment.

11 A Japanese fishing vessel far from the explosion was showered with radioactive ash—fallout from the nuclear cloud. Unaware of the nature of the poison, the men returned to their home port. All were seriously affected, and many died.

That argument, which completely discounts the calculation of the consequences, can today be reinforced by another which is not without significance. It is a truism that there have been great changes in the methods of waging war in the last decade. In 1939, it was my judgment—perhaps I was wrong, but I thought it right at the time—that all the worst that could be done to the human race by the sort of war that seemed probable in the 1940s could not exceed the damage which would have been done to the human race by the world victory of Nazism.

I am not sure that a comparable judgment could be made today. We look, of course, at what is worst in Communism, and we are apt to forget some of its material achievements. I think, perhaps, that is no worse than the attitude of those who look only at the material achievements and quite forget what is bad and evil in it. What is evil—if one thinks of it extending over the whole earth and lasting many years, perhaps decades—is a daunting prospect. But it would not last for ever.

To confine the spirit of man within a spiritual straitjacket for ever is absolutely inconceivable. All I have to say is that it is not a self-evident proposition that the damage done to the human race now, and in the centuries in the future, by the world victory of Communism would be worse than the damage done to the human race by a hydrogen-bomb war fought in order to prevent it.

Now I will pass to some much more practical considerations, and I would say that these are the ones which, in the end, decisively move me. I want to stick as closely as I can to purely strategic considerations, to the problems of defending this country and sustaining the peace of the world for the next 25 or 50 years. But it is very difficult to confine oneself to what are strictly called strategic, let alone tactical, arguments; for the fact which emerges—and this was confirmed in part by the speech of the hon. and gallant Member for Macclesfield—is that there is no defence in weapons today.

There is no way of saving ourselves unscathed through the next quarter-century or half-century by the disposition of this weapon or of that, or by the adoption of one or the discarding of another. The fact is that, in the new conditions of warfare, strategy has become policy and there is no other long-term strategy except policy.

Here, then, let us come to some of these strategic facts of our situation. We now say, quite openly, that what we rely on to save the peace of the world is the deterrent—the H-bomb—and it is this which makes a decisive difference compared with the situation a year ago. It makes a difference particularly in relation to the problem of co-operation with our American friends, a point which was touched upon by my right hon. and learned Friend the Member for Rowley Regis and Tipton (Mr. A. Henderson).[12]

Twelve months ago was the last occasion on which, in the last resort, we were relying for the defence of the free world upon men on the ground; armed men—some, maybe, armed with atomic artillery. But the essence of the defence of the free world, as we conceived it 12 months ago, was by men on the ground. When we consider men—and in part of this Estimate we are doing so—the fact is that Western Europe has far more men than the United States. It would have been churlish, it would have been intolerable, to suggest, when defence depended on men on the ground, that the United States should provide all the men and Western Europe none. That would have been a fantastic suggestion.

But now the situation is entirely different. For the defence of the free world now and henceforth we count on the deterrent. In this connection, the United States of America

12 Arthur Henderson, who had been Air Minister in the Attlee cabinet, was certainly not anti-American, nor did he oppose the deterrent theory as a temporary measure. Nevertheless, earlier in the debate he had said, "The safety of the human race cannot be entrusted for long to the dangerous and precarious equipoise of the forces of mutual destruction. . . . Salvation can be found in the long run only by taking out of the hands of all governments the means of bringing inescapable doom down upon us all." [Hansard's] *Parliamentary Debates* [Commons] 5th ser., 538 (1955): 660.

—far from being, as it is in terms of manpower, smaller than Western Europe—is fantastically larger in its industrial capacity; in its power of producing aircraft and other weapons, and, of course, fantastically larger still in its taxable capacity.

Even were that not so, the fact stands out that the United States alone, without any assistance from anybody, has got the whole of the deterrent that is needed. Whereas when the matter ultimately depended on men, the United States rightly asked, and insisted, that others concerned should make their contribution in men, the United States—so far as I know—does not even want us to make any contribution to the thermo-nuclear deterrent. The Americans have got enough of it themselves in their own country.

I do not know whether all hon. Members have read the remarkable article by Cassandra in the "Daily Mirror" of 24th February. I confess that I should normally expect to find deeply significant articles more frequently in the "Manchester Guardian" or "The Times" than in the "Mirror." But when we find them in the "Mirror," they are not less impressive for that.[13] Our friend, Mr. Connor, paid a visit to the headquarters of the American strategic bomber force. He had the advantage of being shown round and of discussing its present strength and problems and intentions in a big way.

Among other things, he wrote:

"The spearhead of strategic air command is over 1,200 B 47 six-jet bombers and swiftly increasing reinforcements of the new B 52 eight-jet bomber . . . the B 47 is . . . capable of carrying the hydrogen bomb . . . at over six hundred miles an hour at . . . nearly fifty thousand feet. And its range—by being refuelled in mid-air . . . can take it to any part of the Soviet Union—and back."

[13] The *Mirror* is a popular tabloid, whereas *Guardian* and *Times* are conservatively written with many carefully prepared analytical articles. Are there parallels in American papers?

What has the R.A.F. in being, or in prospect, which can compare for one moment with that? What have we in prospect, in three or in five years time, which will compare with what this will by then have grown into? And what are they doing?

Reading between the lines—one does not have to go very far between the lines, one can read the actual plain meaning of the words—it is pretty clear that the American's strategic bomber force has already photographed every square mile of the Soviet Union by night, at over 50,000 feet, with infra-red photography. There they are, in fact, poised and ready.

And then come these words:

> "I questioned General LeMay on the possibilities of a 'preventive war.' He would express no direct opinion, but said that when it comes to trading knock-out punches . . . it might not be the best policy to sit and wait until you are hit so hard that you never wake up again."

We in the West naturally have fears—justified or not I will not argue—that some time, when it suits their case, and when they think they can get away with it, the leaders of the Soviet Union may launch an unlimited military assault upon us. But were one a Russian responsible for policy, and were one to read that article, might not a slight cold shiver travel up and down one's spine?

At any rate, the position is that here are these two giants. They threaten each other with complete extermination. The American Air Force is quite sufficient to carry out the threat of complete extermination if need be. To that possibility the R.A.F. of today, and even the maximum possible R.A.F. that we could build by concentrating all our economic resources upon it, would make a hardly significant addition.

I must turn aside for a moment to deal with one argument which has been particularly prevalent amongst hon. Members on this side of the House. It has been stated that in some curious way the possession of a strategic bomber force armed with hydrogen bombs will make us independent of the Americans. That is the most extraordinary argument that I have ever heard. I hope that you, Sir, and the House will allow me time to spell out the strategic nonsense of it, because if by the possession of strategic bombers armed with hydrogen bombs we make Britain independent of the United States we must mean one or both of two things.

We must either mean that with our bomber force we could threaten the U.S.S.R. with the ultimate deterrent, even if the United States stood passively by; or we must mean that if the U.S.A. got itself into the position of exchanging hydrogen punches with Russians in circumstances of which we did not approve, we should have the power to keep out. But surely if we examine either of these propositions we shall find that neither can be maintained for a single moment.

It is a very unpopular thing to say anything which reminds us of how small is our island. But can anyone in this House get up and tell me that, with the U.S.A. standing neutral, we could sit across from a tough Russian negotiator at a conference table and say to him, "If you do not give way to us then we are going to drop our hydrogen bombs on you"? In a hydrogen-bomb war, with the Americans out, and with Britain fighting the U.S.S.R. does anyone think that we could annihilate one-quarter of the bases from which the Russians would launch their bomber planes and their rockets before they had destroyed, mainly by short-range rockets, every possibility of organised life here, let alone any possibility of carrying on a military struggle? If it is thought that by possessing a strategic bomber force we make ourselves independent of the Americans in the sense that we could threaten the Russians without the Americans, then I say it is untrue.

What about the other argument? If the Americans and the Russians start trading H-bombs with each other, various countries might have the good luck to escape from the consequences. India might be left out; or Italy or New Zealand might be left out—

Mr. Emrys Hughes: And Ireland.

Sir R. Acland: My hon. Friend says Ireland.

The argument that I am going to advance now is one of a relatively lower level of national selfishness, but I offer it all the same. We might be left out if we have not a strategic bomber force or the hydrogen bomb. But if we have a strategic bomber force and the hydrogen bomb, which cannot add 5 per cent. to the strength of the American onslaught, one thing is absolutely certain—that we shall, from the first day, be in any hydrogen-bomb war into which the Russians and the Americans get themselves.[14]

I must, I am afraid, pick out one argument used by the Prime Minister in the course of his speech in the debate on defence, because it seems to me an argument which anyone of his strategic capacity ought to have seen through. He said that we must have a strategic bomber force of our own in order that, if the hydrogen-bomb war started, we should be in the happy position of picking and choosing our targets and of not having to rely on the Americans to bomb targets for us.

With great respect to the right hon. Gentleman, that is irrelevant. Let anybody advance to me an argument about the kind of weapons which we might need for the kind of cold war action such as in Korea, which might take place again without leading to the hydrogen bomb; such an arrangement[15] is relevant. Let anybody offer in argument the idea that this course or that course could make the use of the hydrogen bomb less likely or more likely, and I say that

[14] After the inauguration of the Campaign for Nuclear Disarmament, this argument was frequently advanced by the unilateralists. In American discussions of nuclear armaments, the parallels would be the revulsion provoked by the concept of "overkill" and the suggestion of placing antiballistic missiles near cities.

[15] Apparently, Acland means to use the word "argument" rather than "arrangement" here.

is also a relevant argument. But to start offering apparently as a decisive argument a calculation based on what happens if and after the hydrogen war itself has broken out, is irrelevant, because when it breaks out it does not matter whether we pick and choose the particular targets which the Americans might not have chosen for us. It is the end.

In passing, may I repudiate the idea that a hydrogen-bomb war would mean the end of the human race. In some parts of the world men would survive, and although they might have to revert to infanticide to rid the world of monsters, they would none the less survive. But not for us. If this war breaks out and we are in it, that is the end for us.

That brings me back to the question of how to stop it, and here in the short run I accept the answer that was given in the defence debate by the Prime Minister. In the short run, the hope of not having a hydrogen-bomb war rests in our belief that these two giants, counterpoised against each other in hatred, fear, power, and suspicion, may each be so terrified of the damage that might be done by one to the other than neither will take the responsibility of unleashing the final holocaust. That is a real hope, though not a certainty, in the short run.

But what about the long run? How long has the human race to live on this razor edge of tension, with the minds of our young men in schools and universities—as hon. Members must know it in cases of their own children—distorted through the domination of their lives by this fear which hangs over all of us? How long is it to go on? Surely the only relevant, strategic question is, what line of policy can we possibly adopt which will give us some chance—I do not say a certainty because we cannot say "certainty" in these matters—to play our part in relaxing, over the decades, this tension between these two giants which strains the world to distraction.

Consider the U.S.A. and the U.S.S.R. in isolation, and assume, for the purposes of argument, the hypothetical case that they are the only two nations in the world. I would say that in such a situation there could be no long-term hope for the relaxation of the tension at all. It exists between these two great Powers, and nothing that can happen so far as either of them is concerned will ever begin to lessen the tension.

I say, not in hatred or even in criticism of the people or the Government of the U.S.S.R. or those of the U.S.A., but just because of the nightmare situation in which they find themselves, that, as far as those two giants are concerned in their relations with each other, there is no possibility, except a continuance of fear, distrust, power to meet fear, more fear because of more power, more hatred because of more fear, more distrust and more tension.

Therefore, the only hope of the world and for our children and grandchildren lies in this: that some other peoples, extending at each moment the very maximum of tolerance, sympathy, and understanding, and, of course, constructive criticism, both to America and to the U.S.S.R., may be able, over the course of years, to show those two giants the way of learning to tolerate each other. India has done a little of this essential work within the last couple of years.

I do not want to whitewash the Indians completely as if they were saints. Alas, their relations with their nearest neighbours are sometimes open to criticism, whether it be valid or not. But in relation to the great world and to the tension between East and West, the Indians, in the last 12 months or two years, have achieved something.

I will add something more. The Foreign Secretary achieved something in relation to the conflict in Indo-China. Let me point out, however, in relation to the question whether we need to possess power in order to achieve such results, that the right hon. Gentleman achieved this success before we were committed to building the hydrogen bomb and a strategic air force; and, much more important, he achieved his success after it had become clear that we were not in any circumstances going to use force in relation to the Indo-China conflict.

By embarking now upon the building of the strategic bomber force, which has no purpose except to carry the hydrogen bomb, we place ourselves for ever—or at least until this decision is reversed—outside the arena from which we could be effective in assuaging the ghastly tension between the two great countries which tears the heart out of mankind. By making ourselves an integral part of one of the two poles between which the tension rages, we can do nothing more to relieve it.

All our actions from now on will only serve to intensify fear, hate, power, and suspicion. We are handing over the task of assuaging the tension to others, such as Sweden, India, Indonesia, and a few more. My fear is that without us those others are not quite strong enough to succeed. If we pursued the strategic policy necessary to join them I believe that we and they together might bring it off.

I hope you will forgive me, Mr. Speaker, for ending by making a few personal points. My arguments, such as they are, are not, of course, strengthened in any way by anything that I intend to do about them. They deserve only such attention as they can earn on their merits. No man will expect, in a large organisation, that everybody will always agree with him. Often he has to vote in a minority, and then shrug and go along with colleagues whom he trusts but who take a view different from him.

To each, however, there is bound to come a time when he has to say to his friends that here he has come to an issue that he feels to be so decisive that he cannot keep company with them any longer with only such mild protests as a speech, a Motion on the Order Paper, and perhaps an occasional naughty vote in a Lobby which the Whips suggest to be the wrong one. The time must come when he has to stand up and take the final step and say, reluctantly, "On this issue we must part company and I must test out what the electors feel about it."

I would say to my constituents, if I could, that I understand the difficulties which I shall impose upon them. Indeed, the prospect of that has been by far the strongest argument which might have deterred me from the course which I am pursuing.

But at this time, when I am sure that many little people are bewildered by the fact that both the leading parties have accepted this horror and—if I may say so with all friendship—when the initiative taken by my right hon. Friend the Member for Ebbw Vale (Mr. Bevan) in the defence debate last week was, to say the least of it, so bewildering[16] somebody must go to the limits of what is possible within the framework of our democracy in order to assert that reconciliation, sympathy and understanding—even sympathy and understanding for men and nations that we believe to be wrong—are, in the end, stronger and more decisive forces than anything that comes out of the instruments of unlimited physical power. I should not be true to myself if I did anything other than that.

QUESTIONS AND REFERENCES

1. Sir Richard Acland's speech may be evaluated within the framework set forth in Chapter One, pp. 14–15. Because the speech received extensive press coverage, its audience consisted not only of the assembled members of the House of Commons but of his constituents in Gravesend and all of the British people. How does he adapt his arguments to each segment of his audience?

2. If you had been a member of Parliament hearing this speech, to what extent would you have been able to identify with Sir Richard in the point of view he sets forth? Would your party affiliation have made a difference? your attitude toward the H-bomb? How would you have reacted if you had been a British writer on political and social questions? How would you have reacted as an ordinary member of the British public?

3. What are the major arguments advanced in the speech? Evaluate the quality of the reasoning and the supporting material used. Are there any especially moving passages? What is the source of the feeling they invoke?

[16] Aneurin Bevan had spoken eight days earlier in a debate on defense policy. In this speech, he had seemed unable to decide whether he was for or against the H-bomb. The speech foreshadowed the position he was to take in his celebrated speech before the Labour Party Conference in 1957. See pp. 41–54.

4. What impression do you get of Sir Richard Acland as a man? Does this in any way affect your acceptance or rejection of his ideas?

5. Acland presents an urgent problem in his question "How long has the human race to live on this razor edge of tension, with the minds of our young men in schools and universities . . . distorted through the domination of their lives by this fear which hangs over all of us?" Is this fear a factor in the worldwide alienation of youth from their elders? Specifically, is it important to students on your campus? What does it mean to you as an individual? Would a genuine peace settlement significantly change the attitudes of your fellow students as well as your own? How?

6. For a later statement of Acland's views, see his book *Waging Peace* (London: Frederick Muller, Ltd., 1958), in which he argues that on both practical and moral grounds nuclear war is unthinkable. Since Acland's views have a religious basis, you might wish to compare a series of Catholic essays representing diverse views. See Walter Stein (ed.), *Nuclear Weapons and Christian Conscience* (London: Merlin Press, Ltd., 1961).

Naked to the Conference Table

ANEURIN BEVAN

From the inception of antinuclear agitation, it was apparent that the political hopes of the protesters lay of necessity in the Labour party. Sentiment against the use of the bomb was in a minority in that party, but it was nearly nonexistent among Conservatives. Left wing Labour members had taken an independent line on both domestic and foreign issues, pushing for more rapid nationalization and for freedom from American influence. At times this independence took the form of defying the party whips by abstaining or even voting against party-line motions. The voice of the dissidents was the weekly journal, Tribune, *and their most influential parliamentary spokesman was the irrepressible Aneurin Bevan. Twice in the postwar period he was disciplined by the party leadership, but in each case the party's need for a powerful voice in the House of Com-*

mons and Bevan's need for a secure party base resulted in an uneasy reconciliation.

The Tribune group accepted Bevan as their natural leader, and soon the rebels were dubbed Bevanites by the press. The pressure they exerted pushed the party leadership to adopt a position favoring the suspension of atomic tests, and the Bevanites pressed for an additional step—a declaration that under a Labour government Britain would not be the first to use the bomb. Although such a position made nonsense of the Dulles deterrent theory, Bevan stopped short of a demand for unilateral abandonment of nuclear weapons. But because his position was somewhat ambiguous, many of the left wingers believed that he would eventually come to advocate unilateralism.

At conference time (a policy conference normally held each year) the leadership could always count on the bloc votes of the big unions to sustain a cautious policy. In particular they counted on the vote of the huge Transport and General Workers Union (TGWU), headed by the conservative Arthur Deakin. Upon Deakin's death, however, the TGWU took a sharp turn to the left with the election of Frank Cousins as head of the union. On the question of nuclear weapons Cousins leaned toward the unilateralist position, but vacillated in his advocacy until after the CND became strong.

After Bevan had been disciplined by the party for going against the official line in 1955, he had challenged Hugh Gaitskell first for the position of party treasurer and then for the leadership when Clement Attlee retired. By 1957, however, he had made his peace with Gaitskell, given up his aspirations to the top party post, and accepted positions in the Gaitskell shadow cabinet—first as spokesman for colonial affairs and then as spokesman for foreign affairs. The Bevanites feared he had sold out to the party leadership; they felt that this was confirmed by his speech at the Brighton Conference in 1957. Bevan himself, however, for whatever motivation, had come to believe that the important thing was to obtain power, and that if he should *become foreign minister he could persuade both the Americans and the Russians to modify their positions on nuclear warfare. For this reason he further diluted whatever unilateralist sentiment he had and made the speech at the Brighton Conference that diverted the Labour party's trend toward unilateralism but alienated the Bevanites from their leader. Cousins, who had come to the Conference with the intention of voting for a unilateralist resolution, was moved by the speech to request time for the delegates to reconsider their positions, and he eventually cast his vote with Bevan for the position favored by the party executive.*

The Executive Committee had a discussion about these composite resolutions, and at first it was thought that perhaps it would be better for the Executive to make an opening statement and also a winding-up statement as has been done on other occasions this week. But in order to give the Conference itself an opportunity of expressing its own views as long as possible it was decided to leave the Executive statement until the end. I cannot help thinking that it was a slightly unfortunate decision, because so far the discussion has taken a form which is in grave danger of falsifying the whole issue. There is no member of the Executive in favour of the hydrogen bomb. To state the argument as though we are divided among people who support the hydrogen bomb and those who are against the hydrogen bomb is completely to falsify the argument. If the Executive had asked me to get up on this platform this morning and support the hydrogen bomb I would have refused. I have made probably more speeches to more people condemning the hydrogen bomb than anybody in this conference, and I am as strongly against the hydrogen bomb now as ever I was. So for heaven's sake do not get into a false antithesis.

Let us get the argument straight. It is an unfortunate fact that composite resolutions are apt to be clumsy instruments. There is no other way of getting things before the conference, but in our own experience over and over again we have found that when we are composited we find ourselves often in strange company and we find that we are having to vote for things with which we disagree in order to vote for the things with which we agree. Also we have to vote for resolutions which appear to say what they want and say it on the surface, but which contain implications which are not always understood.

What has been the attitude of this movement so far towards this problem? Our attitude has been expressed in a resolution that was carried at the Socialist International in Vienna. We are not committed to that resolution because resolutions have to be adopted by the Socialist parties of the member states before they become instruments of national policy. But nevertheless we did state our position and as the resolutions were drafted by the British delegates we are to some extent committed to them. What did we say? The first statement we made at Vienna was that the proposals that at that time had been advanced by the Soviet Union for the cessation of nuclear tests should be accepted. We have gone further than that and we have said not only should they be accepted but that if there is a Socialist Government in Great Britain, Britain will take the initiative in suspending all tests. Why did we say that? For two reasons. First, for reasons that have been advanced this morning, to give a unilateral lead to the world; because we were tired of the endless disarmament conferences which aborted each other and from which nothing was coming at all. So we said one of the powers must give a lead. Therefore we decided the lead must be given by Great Britain. We decided that because we consider that it is an immoral thing for a nation to make tests which poison not only its own nationals but the nationals of other peoples. We consider that there is something profoundly wrong about behaviour of that sort and that therefore we should not be parties to it.

We also thought that by a decision of that sort and by carrying it out other nations would be brought to follow our example. One advantage about the suspension of tests which does not belong to the other parts of resolution 24 is that when you decide to suspend tests it can be found out whether you are keeping your word. That is the important point about suspending the tests. The great difficulty about the disarmament discussions is that the nations do not trust each other. That is why they talk so much about systems of mutual inspection because although nations may say things other nations will not believe that they are doing what they are saying. I am bound to tell this Conference that the reputation of Great Britain in the councils of the world since the Suez incident does not necessarily mean that we should be believed. But we would be believed if we decided to suspend the tests because that fact could be found out.

It has been said this morning, quite rightly, that the suspension of the tests would itself mean, so long as they were suspended that we would not be able to go on making nuclear weapons. That is all right, isn't it? Nothing wrong with that, is there? It meets both points, doesn't it? What we would then be hoping for, very much hoping for, is that in the climate of opinion created by that fact it would be possible for the other countries to follow our example and by the relaxation of tension that would be then produced we could proceed to further stages of disarmament.

One of the great difficulties about the talks in the past has been that they have attempted to put too much in the package deal which other nations would not accept. What we decided at Vienna was that it was far better to act where agreement was possible than postpone any action until more agreement had been reached. In other words we said, if you try to go too far you will get nowhere, but if you do take practical action on a limited area of agreement, when that has been accomplished further action may become possible. That is what we decided after very serious consideration.

We also decided in Vienna that we did not believe in the British Government's policy of linking up disarmament with political settlements, because we considered that such a device merely tended to prevent disarmament and also prevent reaching the settlements. Obviously if you cannot reach a political settlement the nations will not proceed with disarmament, and they will not proceed with disarmament because they have not settled. Therefore when Macmillan in his answer to Bulganin stated that the British Government in concert with the Western German Government and the Americans were not prepared to proceed to further stages of disarmament until political settlements had been reached, particularly in Europe, we pointed out that that could only mean one thing, and that was that arms were being kept in the background as a sanction to compel political settlements. We decided, therefore, that those must be divorced one from the other. So our disarmament policy in that respect has been established.

May I repeat again that the suspension of tests means a suspension of production, and in the atmosphere created by it we would try to proceed to further stages by agreement with the Soviet Union and the United States.

The great difficulty about composite No. 24 is that what it will mean does not appear on the surface of the resolution.[17] I do not believe that this conference ought to resolve all fundamental issues of British international relationships and British foreign policy as an incidental by-product of a resolution. Let me explain what I mean. You may decide in this country unilaterally that you will have nothing to do with experiments, nor with manufacture, nor with use. With none of those sentiments do I disagree, none of them at all. But you can't, can you, if you don't want to be guilty, appear to be benefiting by the products of somebody else's guilt? [18] Let me put it more concretely. You will have to say at once—immediately, remember, not presently—that all the international commitments, all the international arrangements, all the international facilities afforded to your

[17] Resolution 24 pledged "that the next Labour Government will take the lead by itself refusing to continue to test, manufacture or use nuclear weapons, and that it will appeal to the peoples of the other countries to follow their lead." (*Report of the Fifty-Sixth Annual Conference of the Labour Party* [London: 1957], p. 165.) There was no mention of NATO or the United Nations.

[18] Bevan is arguing that it would be morally wrong to accept the shelter of the American nuclear deterrent while making a moral argument against its use.

friends and allies must be immediately destroyed. (Cries of 'Why Not?') If you say 'Why not?', then say it in the resolution. It is not said there. It has not been said. (A cry of 'It is implied.') Yes, it is implied, but nobody said it. Everybody argued about the horror that the hydrogen bomb is in reality, but what this Conference ought not to do, and I beg them not to do it now, is to decide upon the dismantling of the whole fabric of British international relationships without putting anything in its place, as a by-product of a resolution in which that was never stated at all. I say that that whole question has been hidden. I know many of my comrades believe that unilateral action of that sort will lead other nations immediately to take action of a similar sort. We can say that about the suspension of tests, but can you say it about all the rest?

I saw in the newspapers the other day that some of my actions could be explained only on the basis that I was anxious to become Foreign Secretary. I am bound to say that is a pretty bitter one to say to me. If I thought for one single moment that that consideration prevented the intelligent appreciation of this problem I would take unilateral action myself, now. Is it necessary to recall to those who said 'Hear, hear' that I myself threw up office a few years ago? And I will not take office under any circumstances to do anything that I do not believe I should do.

But if you carry this resolution and follow out all its implications and do not run away from it you will send a British Foreign Secretary, whoever he may be, naked into the conference chamber. Able to preach sermons, of course; he could make good sermons. But action of that sort is not necessarily the way in which you take the menace of this bomb from the world. It might be that action of that sort will still be there available to us if our other actions fail. It is something you can always do. You can always, if the influence you have upon your allies and upon your opponents is not yielding any fruits, take unilateral action of that sort. (A cry of 'Do it now.') 'Do it now,' you say. This is the answer I give from the platform. Do it now as a Labour Party Conference? You cannot do it now. It is not in your hands to do it. All you can do is pass a resolution. What you are saying is what was said by our friend from Hampstead, that a British Foreign Secretary gets up in the United Nations, without consultation—mark this; this is a responsible attitude!— without telling any members of the Commonwealth, without concerting with them, that the British Labour movement decides unilaterally that this country contracts out of all its commitments and obligations entered into with other countries and members of the Commonwealth—without consultation at all. And you call that statesmanship? I call it an emotional spasm.

Comrades, if that is what you mean, you ought to have said it, but you have not said it. It has not been said in the resolution at all. It has not been brought out in the debate. It has not been carefully considered. It has all been considered merely as a by-product of an argument about the hydrogen bomb. I am anxious to protect this country from hydrogen bombs.

If we contracted out, if we produced this diplomatic shambles it would not necessarily follow that this country would be safer from the hydrogen bomb. (Cries of 'Nehru has no bomb.') No. Nehru has no bomb, but he has got all the other weapons he wants. Nehru has no bomb, but ask Nehru to disband the whole of his police forces in relation to Pakistan and see what Nehru will tell you.

The main difficulty we are in here is that in this way we shall precipitate a difficult situation with the nations that are now associated with us in a variety of treaties and alliances, most of which I do not like—I would like to substitute for them other treaties more sensible and more civilised and not chaos and a shambles. If any Socialist Foreign Secretary is to have a chance he must be permitted to substitute good policies for bad policies. Do not disarm him diplomatically, intellectually, and in every other way before he has a chance to turn round.

This country could be destroyed merely as an incident of a war between Russia and the U.S.A. It is not necessary for any bombs to drop on us. If war broke out between the U.S.A. and the Soviet Union, this country would be poisoned with the rest of mankind. What we have, therefore, to consider is how far the policies we are considering this morning can exert an influence and a leverage over the policies of the U.S.A. and of the Soviet Union.

I do seriously believe in the rejection of the bomb. But that is not the issue. That is what I am telling you. If resolution 24 only meant that we would have very little difficulty with it. But if resolution 24 is read with its implications it means that as decent folk you must immediately repudiate all the protection and all the alliances and all the entanglements you have with anybody who uses or possesses or manufactures hydrogen bombs. That is our dilemma. I find it a very, very serious dilemma. This problem is without precedent in the history of the world. I consider that it is not only a question of practical statesmanship; I agree with Frank Cousins and all those who have spoken this morning that it is a high moral question, too.

No nation is entitled to try to exterminate an evil by invoking a greater evil than the one it is trying to get rid of. The hydrogen bomb is, of course, a greater evil than any evil it is intended to meet. But, unfortunately, the U.S.S.R. and the U.S.A. are in possession of this weapon, and we are in danger of being exterminated as a consequence of their rivalries and their antagonisms. What I would like to have is the opportunity of exerting influence upon the policies of those countries, but this is not the way to do it. You do not give us a chance. It was said to me during the week, 'What is the use of getting up on the platform and saying you are going to stop or suspend the tests?' We have said that already. Are we thinking merely in terms of stronger and stronger resolutions accompanied by no action at all? If I may be permitted to strike a facetious note, it is like the comedian in the music hall who told his wife he was going to give her a bicycle. 'But,' she said, 'you promised me that the week before and the week before last.' He said, 'I'm a man of my word. I will promise it you next week too.' It is no use here, because we have passed a resolution, to pass a stronger one when the weaker one itself has not been started.

I am begging and praying our comrades here to reconsider the demands they have made, because I agree that those who support resolution No. 24 do it with complete sincerity. They do it because they believe that the resolution embodies their detestation of the bomb. But I am sure that in your secret hearts you will admit that you have not fully thought out the implications of that. You have not realised that the consequence of passing that resolution would be to drive Great Britain into a diplomatic purdah. You have not thought out the fact that we are in relations with other countries. I am speaking not only about Great Britain, but the Socialist Party. You are not entitled, I submit, to take action as a Socialist Government without giving any other members of the Commonwealth any opportunity of considering the implications of the action we ourselves decided to take.

Furthermore, I have tried to make this point and I hope it has been considered. If we decided unilaterally not to make the bomb we should only have been deciding by resolution what would naturally follow from the suspension of tests. Obviously if we decide we will not use the bomb I want you to face up to the fact that unfortunately this sort of weapon is not a weapon you can decide not to use or to use. That is the damnable nature of the bomb. Clem Attlee pointed out in the House of Commons that the great danger of the existence of these deadly weapons is the problem of anticipation. You have already had articles written in the newspapers by soldiers. You had an article the other day in the *Telegraph* in which a soldier pointed out that the decision to use this bomb will never be a decision taken by parliaments; it will not even be a decision taken by cabinets. It may be a decision taken by an individual man who, acting upon some report of some of his spies, maybe by telephone tapping, will have been made to fear that the other chap is going to drop his bomb. (A cry of 'Do not give it to him.')

We do not give it to him. He has got it. And we are not speaking about our bomb, we are speaking about their bomb.

A Voice: Give an example.

Mr. Bevan: All right. We are endeavouring to. I am endeavouring to face you with the fact that the most important feature of this problem is not what we are going to do in this country, because that lies within our control. What we have to discuss is what is the consequence of the action upon other nations with far more deadly weapons than we have. I do beg and pray the conference to reconsider its mood in this matter, and to try and provide us with a workable policy, with a policy which in the consequence I believe will be more effective in getting rid of the bomb than resolution 24 if it is carried.

In fact I would say this; I would make this statement. I have thought about this very anxiously. I knew this morning that I was going to make a speech that would offend and even hurt many of my friends. Of course. But do you think I am afraid? I shall say what I believe, and I will give the guidance that I think is the true guidance, and I do not care what happens. But I will tell you this, that in my opinion, in carrying out resolution 24, with all the implications I have pointed out, you will do more to precipitate incidents that might easily lead to a third world war—(Cries of 'Rubbish,' 'Oh,' and 'Shame'). Just listen. Just consider for a moment all the little nations running one here and one there, one running to Russia the other rushing to the U.S.A., all once more clustering under the castle wall, this castle wall, or the other castle wall, because in that situation before anything else would have happened the world would have been polarised between the Soviet Union on the one side and the U.S.A. on the other. It is against that deadly dangerous negative polarisation that we have been fighting for years. We want to have the opportunity of interposing between those two giants modifying, moderating, and mitigating influences. We have been delighted because other nations are beginning to take more and more independent stands. We are delighted because the Iron Curtain has been becoming more and more pliable. We are delighted because nations of different political complexions are arising. We are delighted because the texture of international relationships is changing. When I met Krushchev a few days ago I told him that as a Marxist he should understand that just as technical changes in society bring about revolutions in social relationships so the technical changes in modern weapons have revolutionised international relationships.

I am convinced, profoundly convinced, that nothing would give more anxiety to many people who do not share our political beliefs than if the British nation disengaged itself from its obligations and prevented itself from influencing the course of international affairs. I know that you are deeply convinced that the action that you suggest is the most effective way of influencing international affairs. I am deeply convinced that you are wrong. It is therefore not a question of who is in favour of the hydrogen bomb and who is against the hydrogen bomb, but a question of what is the most effective way of getting the damn thing destroyed.

Having spent so much time on this I have no time to speak about the other resolutions, but this, I admit, is the most important one of all. Composite No. 19 the Executive accept.[19] Composite No. 20 [20] the Executive ask to have remitted, not because they disagree with the principles, but because they do not consider that when it is read outside it will have enough felicity of expression, and as one document this week has been somewhat misunderstood we do not want it to happen with another. Composite 23 we accept.[21] We are hoping that composite 24 will not be pressed. We are prepared to accept composite No. 25 with the understanding that it means suspension,[22] because suspension in

[19] An omnibus resolution dealing with strengthening the United Nations.
[20] An eleven-point "solution" to Middle Eastern difficulties.
[21] A resolution advocating abolition of nuclear weapons by negotiation.
[22] The word in the resolution is "cessation." How do Bevan's terms for acceptance change the idea?

this case is a more effective instrument to influence the conduct of others. We do not speak about the time of suspension, because how long this suspension should go on for is a practical question and not one of principle; it is a matter of how long the suspension will exert its influence on the behaviour of other nations.

This is the most serious debate. As has been quite properly said, all the other discussions that we have had are of no avail unless the issues proposed in this debate are properly resolved. It is the most difficult of all problems facing mankind. It can be resolved, I agree, only by a combination of resolution and of intellectual belief. I have reached my conclusion after a lot of agonising thinking, and I am convinced deeply of this, that if resolution 24 is adopted with all the implications that I have pointed out it will very gravely embarrass a Socialist Government and may have disastrous consequences throughout the world.

QUESTIONS AND REFERENCES

1. In his autobiographical work, *In Place of Fear*, new ed. (London: Macgibbon and Kee, Ltd., 1961), which also deals with the role of Labour members of Parliament, Bevan states, on page 25, that "the first essential in the pioneers of a new social order is a big bump of irreverence." His reputation was made as the leader of anti-Establishment forces. Evaluate the speech in that light.

2. This speech undoubtedly helped to prevent the Labour party from endorsing unilateralism in 1957. What is there in the speech that contributed to this end? clear statement of idea? adequate supporting material acceptable to the audience? forceful and appealing language? How much of the success of the speech should be attributed to the speaker's ethos (his character, intelligence, and good will) as it was perceived by the audience? Was this recognition entirely antecedent to the speech, or did the speech itself add to the speaker's ethos?

3. Suppose that Bevan had eventually acquired power, as Prime Minister or Defence Minister. On the basis of this speech, do you think that he would have used nuclear weapons to counter:
a. a Russian takeover of West Berlin?
b. a nonnuclear air raid by the Russians on London?
c. a Russian nuclear attack on the United States, but not on Britain?

In the light of your answers to these questions, how would you evaluate Bevan's wish to retain the H-bomb for its value in negotiating with other powers?

4. A useful book for further reading is Sir Stephen King Hall, *Defence in the Nuclear Age* (London: Victor Gollancz, Ltd., 1958). Hall mixes penetrating analysis of the nuclear dilemma with ironic comments like this one, which appears on page 97, about tactical nuclear weapons: "They are trying to conventionalize nuclear energy for military purposes; one might as well endeavor to sanctify the Devil. You either use him or you don't! You cannot enlist him in the firm as a sleeping partner or a technical adviser."

Three

○ ◑ ◐

Birth of the Campaign for Nuclear Disarmament

The complex nature of the peace movement in Britain makes it impossible in a short study to unravel the many strands that contributed to the Campaign for Nuclear Disarmament. It is evident from what has been said that important contributions were made by religious leaders and by conscience-stricken political leaders like Sir Richard Acland and others, particularly in the Labour party.

That the CND took shape when and as it did, however, was the result of forces set in motion in large part by Canon L. John Collins, Victor Gollancz, Lord Bertrand Russell, Kingsley Martin, and J. B. Priestley. Collins and Gollancz had a pamphlet entitled *Christianity and the War Crisis* (London: Victor Gollancz, Ltd.) published in 1950. The pamphlet in itself was hardly radical in its proposals, but it was forcefully written and it stimulated a new wave of discussion among moribund peace groups. Russell, who had advocated the use of the atom bomb against the Russians to force them to accept the Baruch plan of nuclear control in the period just after the war, now reverted to his earlier radicalism and was advocating the total abandonment of the nuclear deterrent. Kingsley Martin, an early antinuclear spokesman, gave more and more encouragement to discussion of the issue in the pages of the *New Statesman*, of which he was the editor.

Britain and the Nuclear Bomb

J. B. PRIESTLEY

It was in the New Statesman *that the article that proved to be the catalyst of the CND was first published. As Canon Collins described it in* Faith Under Fire, *J. B. Priestley's article exposed "the utter folly and wickedness of the whole of the nuclear strategy."* [1]

At the time of the New Statesman *article, Priestley had a reputation as a prolific essayist and playwright, and, along with Canon Collins and Kingsley Martin, he had been identified with reform movements such as the National Campaign for the Abolition of Capital Punishment. He had not, however, been an activist in the various peace movements. Yet the publication of "Britain and the Nuclear Bombs" in the November 2, 1957, issue of the* New Statesman *provoked such a volume of correspondence that Kingsley Martin requested the cooperation of Arthur Goss and Peggy Duff, chairman and executive secretary, respectively, of the National Committee for the Abolition of Nuclear Weapons Tests (NCANWT). In recognition of the need and the opportunity for a broader based and stronger movement, an ad hoc committee was formed including Collins, Russell, and others. The Campaign for Nuclear Disarmament was established as the successor to NCANWT and the coordinating movement for all who desired to have Britain discard nuclear weapons. The intent of the founders was neither to base the CND upon pacifism nor to exclude pacifists. They*

[1] L. John Collins, *Faith Under Fire* (London: Leslie Frewin, Ltd., 1965), p. 302.

*intended to include both religiously and humanistically mo-
tivated people. They were to invite the cooperation of
leaders of any political party while at the same time denying
them leadership in the campaign. The organization was to
be loose, and although CND itself was limited to peaceful
agitation, the members of the Direct Action Committee,
who were committed to more vigorous measures, were nevertheless welcome to participate in the agitational activity
of CND.*

*Because of the great influence of the Priestley article, we
felt that it deserved a place in the study of the rhetoric of
CND. It is not, of course, a speech, but it is polemic rhetoric
of a high order. Neither is it designed for a universal audience. The* New Statesman *is not a journal of mass circula-
tion. Rather, it is intended to influence opinion-makers and
through them to reach a larger audience. Priestley's contribution to the nuclear disarmament controversy was thus
threefold. Primarily, his* New Statesman *article thrust him
into a position of leadership in the organization of CND.
Secondarily, the article stimulated discussion among opinion-makers in the intellectual community and drew influential persons into the movement. Finally, the article exercised
an indirect influence on many thousands of persons who may
not have read it—students and other young people, the
rank and file of the Labour party, and many others reached
by writings in the popular press and by word of mouth.*

*When CND was established, Priestley was logically one
of the speakers at the organizing meeting and at the dozens
of secondary meetings held throughout the country in the
weeks and months that followed. Yet it is the initial impetus given by "Britain and the Nuclear Bomb" that remains his most important contribution to the debate.*

Two events of this autumn should compel us to reconsider
the question of Britain and the nuclear bombs. The first of
these events was Mr Aneurin Bevan's speech at the Labour
Party conference, which seemed to many of us to slam a

door in our faces.[2] It was not dishonest but it was very much a party conference speech, and its use of terms like 'unilateral' and 'polarisation' lent it a suggestion of the 'Foreign Office spokesman'. Delegates asked not to confuse 'an emotional spasm' with 'statesmanship' might have retorted that the statesmanship of the last ten years has produced little else but emotional spasms. And though it is true, as Mr Bevan argued, that independent action by this country, to ban nuclear bombs, would involve our foreign minister in many difficulties, most of us would rather have a bewildered and overworked Foreign Office than a country about to be turned into a radio-active cemetery. Getting out of the water may be difficult but it is better than drowning.[3]

The second event was the successful launching of the Soviet satellite, followed by an immediate outbreak of what may fairly be called *satellitis*, producing a rise in temperature and signs of delirium. In the poker game, where Britain still sits, nervously fingering a few remaining chips, like a Treasury official playing with two drunk oil millionaires, the stakes have been doubled again. Disarmament talks must no.. take place in an atmosphere properly belonging to boys' papers and science fiction, though already charged with far more hysterical competitiveness. If statesmanship is to see us through, it will have to break the familiar and dubious pattern of the last few years. Perhaps what we need now, before it is too late, is not statesmanship but lifemanship.

One 'ultimate weapon', the final deterrent, succeeds another. After the bombs, the intercontinental rockets; and after the rockets, according to the First Lord of the Admiralty, the guided-missile submarine, which will 'carry a

2 The speech Priestley refers to is the one reproduced in Chapter Two. Note how much of the article is devoted directly or indirectly to Bevan's 1957 speech.
3 Priestley is a skilled writer, and much of the impact of the article derives from his coining of quotable phrases. How many such phrases can you find? Are they well clothed arguments, or merely clever use of language? What effect do you think they had on the reader in 1958? Did they help him to identify with the writer and with the cause he advocated?

guided missile with a nuclear warhead and appear off the coasts of any country in the world with a capability of penetrating to the centre of any continent'. The prospect now is not of countries without navies but of navies without countries. And we have arrived at an insane regress of ultimate weapons that are not ultimate.

But all this is to the good; and we cannot have too much of it, we are told, because no men in their right minds would let loose such powers of destruction. Here is the realistic view. Any criticism of it is presumed to be based on wild idealism. But surely it is the wildest idealism, at the furthest remove from a sober realism, to assume that men will always behave reasonably and in line with their best interests? Yet this is precisely what we are asked to believe, and to stake our all on it.

For that matter, why should it be assumed that the men who create and control such monstrous devices *are* in their right minds? They live in an unhealthy mental climate, an atmosphere dangerous to sanity. They are responsible to no large body of ordinary sensible men and women, who pay for these weapons without ever having ordered them, who have never been asked anywhere yet if they wanted them. When and where have these preparations for nuclear warfare ever been put to the test of public opinion? We cannot even follow the example of the young man in the limerick and ask *Who does what and with which and to whom?* The whole proceedings take place in the stifling secrecy of an expensive lunatic asylum. And as one ultimate weapon after another is added to the pile, the mental climate deteriorates, the atmosphere thickens, and the tension is such that soon something may snap.

The more elaborately involved and hair-triggered the machinery of destruction, the more likely it is that this machinery will be set in motion, if only by accident. Three glasses too many of vodka or bourbon-on-the-rocks, and the wrong button may be pushed. Combine this stock-piling of nuclear weapons with a crazy competitiveness, boastful confidence in public and a mounting fear in private, and what was unthinkable a few years ago now at the best only seems unlikely and very soon may seem inevitable. Then western impatience cries 'Let's get the damned thing over!' and eastern fatalism mutters 'If this has to be, then we must accept it'. And people in general are now in a worse position every year, further away from intervention; they have less and less freedom of action; they are deafened and blinded by propaganda and giant headlines; they are robbed of decision by fear or apathy.

It is possible, as some thinkers hold, that our civilisation is bent on self-destruction, hurriedly planning its own doomsday. This may explain, better than any wearisome recital of plot and counter-plot in terms of world power, the curious and sinister air of somnambulism there is about our major international affairs, the steady drift from bad to worse, the speeches that begin to sound meaningless, the conferences that achieve nothing, all the persons of great consequence who somehow seem like puppets. We have all known people in whom was sown the fatal seed of self-destruction, people who would sit with us making sensible plans and then go off and quietly bring them to nothing, never really looking for anything but death. Our industrial civilisation behaving in a similar fashion, may be under the same kind of spell, hell-bent on murdering itself. But it is possible that the spell can be broken. If it can, then it will only be by an immensely decisive gesture, a clear act of will. Instead of endless bargaining for a little of this in exchange for a little of that, while all the time the bargainers are being hurried down a road that gets steeper and narrower, somebody will have to say 'I'm through with all this'.

In plain words: now that Britain has told the world she has the H-bomb she should announce as early as possible that she has done with it, that she proposes to reject, in all circumstances, nuclear warfare. This is not pacifism.[4] There is no suggestion here of abandoning the immediate defence of this island. Indeed, it might well be considerably strengthened, reducing the threat of actual invasion, which is the

4 Compare this with Donald Soper's defense of the pacifist position.

American official and service opinion would be dead against us, naturally. The unsinkable (but expendable) aircraft carrier would have gone. Certain Soviet bases allotted to British nuclear attack would have to be included among the targets of the American Strategic Air Service. And so on and so forth. But though service chiefs and their staffs go on examining and marking the maps and planning their logistics, having no alternative but resignation, they are as fantastic and unreal in their way as their political and diplomatic colleagues are in theirs. What is fantastic and unreal is their assumption that they are traditionally occupied with their professional duties, attending in advance to the next war, Number Three in the world series. But what will happen—and one wrong report by a sleepy observer might start it off—will not be anything recognisable as a war, an affair of victories and defeats, something that one side can win or that you can call off when you have had enough. It will be universal catastrophe and apocalypse, the crack of doom into which Communism, western democracy, their way of life and our way of life, may disappear for ever. And it is not hard to believe that this is what some of our contemporaries really desire, that behind their photogenic smiles and cheerful patter nothing exists but the death wish.

We live in the thought of this prospect as if we existed in a permanent smog. All sensible men and women—and this excludes most of those who are in the *V.I.P.-Highest-Priority-Top-Secret-Top-People Class,* men now so conditioned by this atmosphere of power politics, intrigue, secrecy, insane invention, that they are more than half-barmy—have no illusions about what is happening to us, and know that those responsible have made two bad miscalculations. First, they have prostituted so much science in their preparations for war that they have completely changed the character of what they are doing, without any equivalent change in the policies of and relations between states. Foreign affairs, still conducted as if the mobilisation of a few divisions might settle something, are now backed with push-button arrangements to let loose earthquakes and pestilences and pronounce the death sentences of continents. This leaves us all in a worse dilemma than the sorcerer's apprentice. The second miscalculation assumed that if the odds were only multiplied fast enough, your side would break through because the other side would break down. And because this has not happened, a third illusion is being welcomed, namely, that now, with everything piling up, poker chips flung on the table by the handful, the tension obviously increasing, now at last we are arriving at an acknowledged drawn game, a not-too-stale stalemate, a cosy old balance of power. This could well be the last of our illusions.

The risk of our rejecting nuclear warfare, totally and in all circumstances, is quite clear, all too easy to understand. We lose such bargaining power as we now possess. We have no deterrent to a nuclear threat. We deliberately exchange 'security' for insecurity. (And the fact that some such exchange is recommended by the major religions, in their earlier and non-establishment phases, need not detain us here.) But the risk is clear and the arguments against running it quite irrefutable, only if we refuse, as from the first too many of us here have refused, to take anything but short-term conventional views, only if we will not follow any thought to its conclusion. Our 'hard-headed realism' is neither hard-headed nor realistic just because it insists on our behaving in a new world as if we were still living in an old world, the one that has been replaced.

Britain runs the greatest risk by just mumbling and muddling along, never speaking out, avoiding any decisive creative act. For a world in which our deliberate 'insecurity' would prove to be our undoing is not a world in which real security could be found. As the game gets faster, the competition keener, the unthinkable will turn into the inevitable, the weapons will take command, and the deterrents will not deter. Our bargaining power is slight; the force of our example might be great. The catastrophic antics of our time have behind them men hag-ridden by fear, which explains the neurotic irrationality of it all, the crazy disproportion between means and ends. If we openly challenge this fear, then we might break the wicked spell that all but a few uncertified lunatics desperately wish to see broken, we could begin to restore the world to sanity and lift this nation from its recent ignominy to its former grandeur. Alone, we defied Hitler; and alone we can defy this nuclear madness into which the spirit of Hitler seems to have passed, to poison the world. There may be other chain-reactions besides those leading to destruction; and we might start one. The British of these times, so frequently hiding their decent, kind faces behind masks of sullen apathy or sour, cheap cynicism, often seem to be waiting for something better than party squabbles and appeals to their narrowest self-interest, something great and noble in its intention that would make them feel good again. And this might well be a declaration to the world that after a certain date one power able to engage in nuclear warfare will reject the evil thing for ever.

QUESTIONS AND REFERENCES

1. To whom is Priestley's article addressed? Does he seek to influence public policy directly or indirectly? What is the action he wishes to implement?

2. Is his appeal rational? Is it emotional? Does the use of one kind of appeal preclude the other?

3. Do you think critics are correct when they claim that this article was the catalyst for the unilateral nuclear-disarmament campaign?

4. Examine copies of the *New Statesman* for the years 1955 through 1960. How often do contributors deal with the subject of the threat of nuclear weapons? How many of these contributions are by Priestley? What changes appear in the thrust of the contributions—both those by Priestley and those by others?

CND'S FIRST RALLY

The choice of the word "campaign" to designate the CND was deliberate. None of the originators of the movement envisioned a permanent organization. Canon Collins, who was chosen as chairman, remained active in the movement longer than most. Lord Russell left the presidency of the campaign in 1960 to form a more militant Committee of 100 after a dispute over the proper role of direct action in the CND. Many of the others lost interest or became disillusioned over the tactics of young militants who had been attracted to the organization.

Some who lost interest may have thought that the organization would carry out a campaign in the British sense of the word—a concentrated effort to obtain specific and limited objectives. A British political campaign, for example, is limited to approximately three weeks before an election. Canon Collins, in the first press conference called by the campaign executive committee, indicated that the aim of the organization was a "sharp, virile, and successful campaign to rid Britain of dependence on nuclear weapons, if need be by unilateral action." [7] Ten years later he still held to the same view.[8] In his opinion, if a campaign is not quickly successful, it should be allowed to lapse, and another strike should be made at an appropriate time.

It was this theory that impelled the organizers of the campaign to launch a major propaganda effort aimed at creating a public opinion that would force one or both of the major political parties to take the actions the CND advocated. The propaganda stated:

We shall seek to persuade British people that Britain must:
  (a) Renounce unconditionally the use or production of nuclear weapons and refuse to allow their use by others in her defense.
  (b) Use her utmost endeavor to bring about negotiations at all levels for agreement to end the armaments race and to lead to a general disarmament convention.
  (c) Invite the cooperation of other nations, particularly non-nuclear powers, in her renunciation of nuclear weapons.
Realizing the need for action on particular issues, pending success in its major objectives, Britain must:

7 Christopher Driver, *The Disarmers* (London: Hodder and Stoughton, Ltd., 1964), p. 45.
8 Personal interview, February, 1968.

(a) Halt the patrol flights of planes equipped with nuclear weapons.
(b) Make no further tests of nuclear weapons.
(c) Not proceed with the agreement for the establishment of missile bases on her territory.
(d) Refuse to provide nuclear weapons for any other country.[9]

It was widely recognized that the campaign called for unilateral nuclear disarmament and that these goals were incompatible with NATO or the American alliance.

To launch the campaign, CND took over a booking of Central Hall for February 17, 1958, made previously by the National Committee for the Abolition of Nuclear Weapon Tests. Central Hall is the largest meeting place in Westminster; it is across the square from the Houses of Parliament, a stone's throw from Westminster Abbey, and a short walk from Downing Street. Five thousand people jammed into the hall, and four additional nearby halls were booked for overflow meetings. Many reports indicate that an equal number milled about outside. More than £1,500 was collected in voluntary contributions. George Clark, in a 1963 pamphlet-résumé of CND activity, capsulizes the speeches:

"In the name of Christianity," declared Canon Collins.
"In the name of common humanity," appealed J. B. Priestley.
"In the name of security," reasoned Sir Stephen King-Hall.
"In the name of survival," posed philosopher Russell.
"In the name of morality," cried A. J. P. Taylor.
"In the name of sanity," roared Michael Foot.

Speaker after distinguished speaker hammered home the central purpose of the Campaign. Britain must abandon the Bomb. She must renounce the policy of massive retaliation and lead the world back to peace and progress. Britain must give up nuclear weapons to save her soul as well as her skin.[10]

[9] Driver, *op. cit.*, p. 47.
[10] George Clark, *Second Wind* (London: Campaign for Nuclear Disarmament, 1963), p. 5.

Steps to Nuclear Disarmament

BERTRAND RUSSELL

None of the principal speeches of the organizational meeting have been published in full. Fragments appear in newspapers and periodicals, and there are descriptions available of the effect of the speeches on the audiences. Of the major speeches, the only written text that appears to be available is that by Lord Russell, who spoke from manuscript. In the Russell archives, the manuscript is designated as a "synopsis," and it is possible that Russell expanded on it in delivery. On the other hand, there are handwritten additions and emendations (incorporated into the text given here), which suggests that the speech was given substantially as it stands.

Physically, Russell was not an impressive speaker. The strength of the speech is to be found in what is said and in the personal prestige of the speaker, not in the delivery. Russell had been imprisoned during World War I for anticonscription activity, and he had a long record of opposition to militarism. Because his aversion to Hitlerism was greater than his aversion to war, he supported World War II. After the war, in the hope of bringing the atomic bomb under international control, he advocated threatening the Soviet Union with bombing unless the Soviet government accepted the Baruch plan for international control. Little by little, however, he became convinced that the superpowers had no intention of controlling nuclear armament, and he joined the unilateral disarmament camp, rapidly becoming one of its most radical proponents.

Throughout his long life Russell engaged in the advocacy of advanced social causes while simultaneously building a monumental reputation as a philosopher and mathematician. In whatever he did, he was out of step with popular opinion, intolerant of views differing from his own, and unable to submit to the slow and tedious process of discus-

sion and group decision. He was thus unable to understand why the great powers are unable to agree on such a simple truth as that "our common interest in human survival" is an obvious basis for discarding nuclear weapons. Russell's speech is an illustration of a rational mind dealing with an irrational problem. He is at his best when stating in cold facts the irrefutable truths about nuclear devastation. His solution also has a logical base. The weakness of the speech lies in the absence of a practical program for the implementation of his ideas.

The world at present is rushing towards disaster. At present it seems an even chance whether any human beings exist forty years hence. If man is to survive, the trend must be reversed. A number of measures will be necessary, some fairly easy, others very difficult. I will take the easiest measures first.

I. *Nuclear Tests Must Be Stopped.*

The harm that is being done by tests is not generally realized, especially as it is cumulative. Sea and rain, in most parts of the world, have become radio-active in varying degrees. In Japan 10 days after Bikini rain was 5000 times as radio-active as before. And unfortunately animals and plants concentrate the radio-active material and become in some cases 50,000 times more infected than the water and soil upon which they depend. The U.S. Navy, in the neighbourhood of Bikini, found some giant clams which they had examined were 2000 times as radio-active as the water in which they lived. The most dangerous substance resulting from nuclear tests is Strontium 90, which is an artificial substance owing its existence wholly to nuclear explosions. It is now found in all parts of the world. It is in all milk. It attacks bones especially and causes cancer as well as mutations of genes which are almost always harmful. *The British Atomic Scientists' Association* calculates that the Bikini test probably caused some 50,000 cancers. How many mental defectives they will cause to be born, it is yet impossible to guess. If you give one man cancer or cause one child to be born an idiot, you are a monster; but if you do the same injury to 50,000, you are a patriot. It is odd that the same Governments which promote expensive research to combat cancer, also employ still more expensive methods of increasing it. Although Great Britain is far removed from all the places where tests have taken place, Strontium 90, in continually increasing quantities, has been found in this country in grass and milk. Each test increases this amount. The tests, if continued, will kill all fish, make meat and milk poisonous, and cause genetic damage which will continue through thousands of years if the race survives. It is politically easy to stop the tests, because they cannot be concealed. Dr. Teller, an atomic physicist in the employ of the American Government, maintains that tests can be concealed, but, so far as I have been able to discover, this opinion is not shared by any experts not in Government pay. I believe it completely possible to stop the tests by agreement. If agreement should not prove possible, Great Britain alone should abandon tests. It is intolerable that our country should be an accomplice in this vast atrocity.

II. *The Danger of a Great War by Accident Must Be Minimized.*

As we have lately learnt, planes carrying H-bombs are continually flying over Great Britain. The Prime Minister has assured us that this involves no new danger since, if the planes crash, the bombs will not explode. This, though perhaps literally true, is a misleading statement.[11] *The New Scientist,* on January 2, pointed out that the bombs carry Plutonium which, even in the absence of a full explosion,

---

[11] The crash of a United States Air Force plane with several H-bombs aboard in Palomares, Spain, early in 1966, gave additional substance to Russell's remark. See Flora Lewis, *One of Our H-bombs Is Missing* (New York: McGraw-Hill, 1967).

would cause very grave damage. It is a highly poisonous substance of which *0.6 millionth of a gram* is considered the largest permissible dose. Like Strontium, it seeks bones. As its half-life is 24,000 years, its escape would mean that a large area would have to be evacuated for a long time, and all cattle and vegetables in the area would have to be destroyed. This, however, is not the gravest danger due to planes carrying H-bombs. A much graver danger is that of accidents mistakenly attributed to enemy action, which might easily precipitate a great war that no one had intended. This is the more likely since it is generally assumed that a war would begin with the destruction of capital cities and would have to be carried on without orders from the central Government. Such great military advantages attach to a surprise attack that each side expects the enemy to resort to it. This inevitably reproduces a state of nerves of which the disastrous consequences are immeasurable. Great Britain ought, not only for the good of the world, but even on the narrowest grounds of national interests, to refuse missile bases on its territory. The Defence Minister stated frankly that, in the event of war, the Government could not protect the population, but only missile stations and aeroplane bases. Since it is these that would cause the motive for attack, it is clear that we are safer without them.

III. *The Spread of H-bombs Must Be Stopped.*

Caligula wished that he could exterminate all his enemies with one blow. *He* was thought mad. There are now three Caligulas in the world—Great Britain, U.S., and U.S.S.R. —who actually possess the power that Caligula desired, but, owing to modern progress, *they* are not thought mad. There is a near and imminent prospect that other countries will soon possess H-bombs. France and Germany want them. We must suppose that China will soon think them necessary.[12] Can we doubt that Egypt and Israel will demand "the great deterrent"? Unless measures are taken very soon, every

[12] Since 1968 both France and China have become nuclear powers.

Sovereign State will soon possess H-bombs. This will enormously increase the likelihood of the Great Powers being drawn into war against their will. It is both our duty and our interest to prevent the acquisition of H-bombs by Powers which do not yet possess them. For this reason, if for no other, Great Britain ought to renounce H-bombs and do everything in its power to cause Russia and America to prevent their acquisition by any State which does not yet have them. It would not be at all difficult for Russia and America, if they were in agreement, to secure this result, and such co-operation might be the beginning of better relations.

IV. *Nuclear Weapons Must Be Abandoned Everywhere.*

The talk of "the great deterrent" is plain nonsense. Those who use this argument always go on to say that of course it will not be necessary actually to employ the deterrent. But, if this were really believed, it is obvious that each side would be willing to agree to its abolition. It is, in fact, a futile weapon, since it will destroy those who use it as well as those against whom it is used. There should be an agreement to destroy all stocks of nuclear weapons and to submit to neutral inspection to make sure that the agreement is observed.[13]

V. *Negotiations For a Détente Should Be Entered Into.*

All negotiations in recent years have been more or less insincere. The aim on each side has not been to reach agreement, but to make proposals which are good for propaganda purposes but involve concealed advantages for one's own side. What is needed is a new direction on both sides and a determination, not only to make proposals, but to find compromises which give no net advantage to either side. We are constantly told that there is a risk in negotiating with the Soviet Government. But those who say this overlook the risk involved in not negotiating. The risk involved in not nego-

[13] In this speech Russell stops short of the unilateral position.

tiating is the extermination of the human race. This, surely, is a greater risk than that of some diplomatic advantage to one side or the other. We must hope that this will become obvious both to Russia and to the United States. Each side should abandon abuse of the other side. We are all sinners. No Great Power has the right to cast the first stone. What is needed on both sides is emphasis on our common interest in human survival rather than upon the matters in which our interests are supposed to differ. Whether we wish it or not, the only road to the welfare of each is the welfare of all.

QUESTIONS AND REFERENCES

1. A useful book to aid in understanding Bertrand Russell is Alan Wood, *Bertrand Russell: The Passionate Sceptic* (London: George Allen and Unwin, Ltd., 1957). Wood states on page 74: "Russell's approach to political questions was usually empirical and practical, based on the evidence of the moment and not on *a priori* principles and preconceptions." Do you think this statement is true of Russell's CND speech? In another statement, on page 75, Wood asserts that "He never championed a political cause unless he was moved by a deeply-felt horror of unnecessary human suffering and a determination to fight the folly which produced it." Is this statement true of Russell's speech? Are the two statements compatible?

2. What problems did Russell have in seeking audience identification? How successful was he in overcoming them?

Stand by Humanity

A. J. P. TAYLOR

The choice of A. J. P. Taylor as one of the speakers at the initial mass meeting of CND was a fortunate one. Taylor's conviction of the futility and immorality of nuclear warfare was based on a lifetime of historical writing and research. As a specialist in European, and particularly German, history, he had been led to study the causes and results of the European wars of the twentieth century, which had proved disastrous for all participants. As a sideline, he had published studies of the history of dissent from Britain's foreign policy, beginning with a monograph on John Bright and the Crimean War, and culminating in a lively book published just before the organization of CND, entitled The Trouble Makers, Dissent Over Foreign Policy, 1792– 1939 *(London: Hamish Hamilton, Ltd., 1957).*

Beyond that, however, Taylor was deeply troubled by the bomb itself. Indeed, of all the speeches given on February 17, Taylor's was the one generally acknowledged to be the most moving. As is the case with most of the others, only fragments of the speech persist. In a personal interview[14] Taylor indicated that he had not written out either a manuscript or notes, but that he had expressed in public what he had been thinking and saying in private. He acknowledged that he had been carried away by the stimulus of the crowd and perhaps had been more emotional in his appeal than he had intended. It is a curious footnote to the history of the CND that Taylor spoke frequently at early meetings but eventually left the movement because, in Canon Collins' words, "he thought the rank and file were too emotional."[15]

The text of the speech presented here has been reconstructed by the editors from fragments found in contemporary sources,[16] and it is admittedly only the strongest portion of the speech. However, it has been approved by A. J. P. Taylor as fairly representative of what he said.

What is it we are dealing with? Not an ordinary bomb with effects measured in yards. Not at all. Tests of the H-bomb make it apparent that within three miles of the point of impact, nothing would survive—no life, no buildings—utter and total destruction. For a radius of seven miles more beyond the area of complete devastation, an occasional structure would survive. If the construction of the area was

[14] February, 1968.
[15] Collins, *op. cit.*, p. 345.
[16] *Daily Herald, New Statesman, Tribune,* and Driver, *The Disarmers.*

of flammable materials, a vast further area would be swept by uncontrollable fires. For hundreds of miles around, every living creature would be subjected to lethal fallout, like the Japanese fishermen in the Pacific. A million lives would be snuffed out at the moment of the explosion, a million more would die painfully over a period of weeks. Those who supposed themselves lucky to survive would beget children born blind, or mentally defective, or grotesque monsters. (A long and dramatic pause).

Is there anyone here who would want to do this to another human being? (Pause—no answer). Then why are we making the damned thing? (Applause and uproar).

You and I must bear the responsibility for these weapons. No one will save us but ourselves. Is humanity so degraded that a lead for right is bound to fail? We should stop at nothing to bring this thing to an end. In the days of agitation for woman suffrage, the suffragettes used to interrupt the speeches of cabinet members with shouts of "Votes for women." Let us follow their example and ensure that no politician of any party can appear on a platform if he supports this military policy without being similarly branded, "Murderer." Stand by humanity. Find your task.

QUESTIONS AND REFERENCES

1. Like Priestley, Taylor is a frequent contributor to the *New Statesman*. Check the issues from 1955 to 1960 for his contributions, noting any changes in his attitude toward CND and unilateralism.

2. What do you think Taylor may have said in the portion of his speech that has been lost? Are there arguments elsewhere in this book that fit the pattern he sets here?

3. Of the three selections in this section, which one makes the best case against the H-bomb? Do the arguments convince you that it should be abandoned by international agreement? by unilateral British action?

4. What is there about Taylor's speech that created a tremendous audience response, whereas other speakers were merely greeted with polite approval? Specifically, compare Taylor's speech with Lord Russell's speech.

Four

● ● ●

The Contest for the Labour Party

From its inception CND was torn by a dispute over methods. A majority of the founders, headed by Canon Collins, Kingsley Martin, and J. B. Priestley, believed in a democratically oriented campaign designed to change British public opinion and force political action to get rid of the nuclear deterrent. A substantial minority, however, headed eventually by Bertrand Russell, believed that only through direct action could results be obtained. Collins believed that although sit-downs and disruptions might get public attention in a way that meetings and marches could not, they would ultimately result in violence and loss of sympathy from the centers of power he wished to influence.

Collins' strategy, which CND followed in the main in its first two years, was for CND to "gear itself to the realities of Britain's parliamentary democracy. . . ." He stated, "The British political set-up being what it was, I believed that one of our first aims should be to win a majority for CND policy within the Labour Party, and a second, so to put the case for British nuclear disarmament to the British public as a whole that, at a general election, a Labour Party committed to our policy could be returned to power." [1]

That the policy had a chance of acceptance was indicated by the existence within the Labour party of a strong minority left wing, firmly committed to the unilateral policy. Within the parliamentary party, there were such perennial rebels as Fenner Brockway, Emrys Hughes, Harold Davies, and Sidney Silverman; there were also newcomers, such as Frank Allaun. Many of the members of this minority left wing appeared at CND meetings as speakers, although CND policy was to limit their influence in official councils. None of them occupied leading roles in the party, but they were important links in CND's chain of influence. Outside of Parliament the left wing dominated an important weekly journal, *Tribune,* and the strong voice of this publication quickly joined in supporting the CND cause. *Tribune,* unlike the influential daily newspapers, reported campaign activities fully, and in its editorials, it promoted CND goals. *Tribune* writers also contributed commentaries to the *Herald,* a Labour-oriented daily, and their influence was extended to some extent through feature stories in the *Guardian.* The importance of *Tribune,* however, is in the degree of influence it was able to exercise within the Labour party itself, to which its primary appeal was directed.

Massive Retaliation Is Massive Nonsense

For this reason, it seemed appropriate to include an editorial commentary from Tribune *in this analysis of rhetoric dealing with the antinuclear debate. This passage appeared in the issue of May 2, 1958. As in the case of the* New States-

[1] L. John Collins, *Faith Under Fire* (London: Leslie Frewin, Ltd., 1965), p. 326.

man *article, this is not a speech, but a powerful written ar-*
gument. It is directed against Conservative party policy on
the bomb. It prudently avoids stating that the Labour party,
if returned to power, would not be likely to act differently.
Rather, by implication, it invites the leaders of the Labour
party to seize upon an exploitable issue and commit them-
selves to the CND unilateral nuclear-disarmament position.
Doubtless the Tribune *commentator knew there was no*
chance that the party would take such a position in 1958 or
in the election year of 1959, but he believed that it was im-
portant to look ahead—to stimulate the discussion and con-
troversy that might persuade the party at a later date.

Britain has begun another round of nuclear tests. As usual,
the flash is shrouded in a cloud of cant.

Each explosion will be "highly successful" and "very useful." The fall-out, of course, is "negligible." This means
that only a few hundred people, perhaps only a few score,
are to die.

Mr. Macmillan's speech last week, devoted to justifying
the tests, set the tone. Students of nuclear double-talk will
have culled from it a few choice items.

New Series

For one thing, officially this will not be a new series, but the
same one. "So far," says the Prime Minister, "we have had
four megaton explosions in our current series." The fact
that it is ten months since the last one makes no difference.
If the Russians give up tests, that is because they have *com-
pleted* a series; we are being asked to *interrupt* a series,
which is obviously not fair.

Then, the tests will be held "unless and until other international agreements make them unnecessary." In reality,
they are to take place well before the summit conference (if
it ever happens) at which such agreements could be reached.

Appropriately delivered to the Primrose League, the
speech gave us another frightening glimpse of the narrow

limits reached by Mr. Macmillan's imagination. Speaking of the Soviet proposal to call off the tests, he said: "This is as if in a football match, one side having scored two goals just before time, asks the opposing team not to play any more."

Not Counted

Is it really the Government's aim to "score" as many tests as possible? Must we go on until we have done as much to poison the atmosphere as the Russians and the Americans, thus proving our greatness and "increasing our influence?"

And what is meant by the phrase: "just before time?" Does the Prime Minister fear that tests will be ended by agreement before we have got into double figures? [2]

Mr. Macmillan aired a few other moth-eaten ideas. "What prevents war," he said (as his predecessors have said just before every war has broken out), "is the balance of power. Peace has been preserved so far, not because the West has disarmed, but because the present balance was roughly equal."

Before the Russians had the hydrogen bomb, the official doctrine was that peace is preserved by the West being ahead. Negotiation from strength, a phrase now quietly dropped, was the foundation of policy. Ruin stared us in the face in the event of the Russians catching up and making the balance equal.

Now the Russians have megaton bombs just like the West. This is an appalling threat, or a guarantee of peace— Mr. Macmillan and Mr. Selwyn Lloyd [3] might be able to decide which, if they didn't make speeches on the same day.

Let us now turn from buffoonery to serious analysis. One of the most thoughtful of American commentators, Mr. Joseph Alsop, writes a candid article on "The New Balance of Power" in this month's *Encounter*.

---

[2] *Tribune's* metaphorical refutation of Macmillan's metaphorical language makes interesting reading. What, if anything, does the exchange establish?

[3] Selwyn Lloyd was Foreign Minister in Macmillan's cabinet.

In a nuclear war, says Alsop, the first blow must be the last. It must be so devastating as to make a counter-blow impossible, for "if there is an exchange of blows in nuclear war, the aggressor will pay for his enemy's destruction with his own destruction—which is too high a price."

But a series of developments, the most important being the long-range missile, have put it beyond the capacity of either side to deliver a blow that would make all retaliation impossible.

If even a fraction of retaliatory power survives, the onslaught has failed. The task is to destroy ALL of the enemy's hundreds of bomber bases or rocket sites, and to do it before the aircraft can be ordered into action or the rockets fired.

Retaliation, of course, does not imply that towns, factories, organised society, or even the civilian population would survive. That is not the point. As Alsop remarks: "It is ironically easier nowadays to destroy another nation than to destroy that nation's power to hit back in its death agony."

To ensure that the decisive blow remains impossible, "structures of nuclear striking power and systems of warning must be continuously maintained and continuously modernised, at constantly increasing expense. There is no escaping this vicious circle of military investment except by international agreement . . . There will be other ghastly stages when anti-missile missiles and satellites with bombs on board come into successive use. Unless there is agreement . . . neither side in the world struggle can ever afford to relax its vigilance."

In fact, as *Tribune* has repeated to the point of monotony, nuclear war means mutual suicide. Hence the danger, which has rightly appalled public opinion, and the essential lunacy of the logic of the H-bomb patrols.

So long as retaliatory power is maintained and Alsop's alternative—agreement—is rejected, the bombers must be kept aloft, ready to do their work whatever happens to the homeland they were once supposed to protect.

But, because their attack cannot be decisive and must indeed bring on general catastrophe, elaborate precautions are taken to recall them in the event of a false alarm.

Clear Sky

It took a public outcry to discover the details of this "Fail Safe" system. As described by Philip Deane in the *Observer,* it is certainly more reliable than we had imagined. However, a war breaking out of a clear sky by sheer accident, though a real possibility, was never the main danger. "Fail Safe" cannot guard against the mounting hysteria of an international crisis.

Angry and harassed rulers are prone to believe in reports of aggression and afraid to wait for confirmation. There is no "Fail Safe" device in the pugnacious soul of a Nixon or a Khrushchev. If he regains his calm in sixteen minutes, that is one minute too many.

What, however, was the purpose for which America and her allies built up their bomber forces? It was to retaliate, not against a nuclear attack, but against a local aggression with ground forces.

The first nuclear blow was to be struck by Strategic Air Command. Mr. Dulles coined the phrase "massive retaliation," as Alsop reminds us, to describe his intended reply to a Chinese landing on Formosa.

The Dulles theory, this candid American observer recognises, "has become a phantasm. Massive retaliation is now massive nonsense. The trouble is that the meanings of those two key words, *deterrent* and *retaliation,* have greatly shrivelled and shrunk in the Eisenhower years. The United States cannot any longer strike the first blow . . . without inviting the annihilation of the U.S. and the West."

Conclusion: "There is no real possibility of nuclear retaliation against non-nuclear action." Alsop takes a far from impossible instance. In a war with Israel, the Arab states are reinforced by Soviet parachutists disguised as "Moslem volunteers" and invited by the Arab governments.

Will the West invite annihilation? No, it will "protest

and wring its hands and do nothing." The same applies to Communist action against Formosa or West Berlin.

Even for those who live in dread of Soviet aggression, the policy of "massive nonsense" gives no comfort. The prospect is that each Soviet advance will leave the West with a choice between surrender and suicide. It is Macmillan and Sandys, and not the Campaign for Nuclear Disarmament, who are leading us into this blind alley.

Led Astray

But in one respect Joseph Alsop is led astray by his own rationality. One major reason why massive retaliation has become impracticable, he thinks, is that America's exposed allies will protest. Confidently he predicts that the European NATO countries "will certainly refuse to provoke their own destruction by permitting Strategic Air Command to strike a first blow."

Alas! our leaders are neither as prudent nor as sensible as Alsop thinks. They still live in the dream-world of "massive nonsense"; the shrivelled words roll as trippingly as ever off their tongues. In the speech just quoted, Mr. Macmillan declared: "Peace depends on the determination to deter, clearly and unambiguously stated."

True, when they get a chance to state their intentions "clearly and unambiguously," they produce only a hesitant stammer. Some faint understanding of the realities penetrates the cloud of cant.

Thus, when Mr. Butler was asked point-blank in a television interview if he would order a nuclear reply to a Russian invasion of Greece, he declined to commit himself, thus making nonsense of the Prime Minister's case (possibly, in his view, merely "the best case we've got.")

Gain Respect

In this pitiable fashion Britain is "increasing her influence" and "gaining the respect" of other nations. The Russians, we are told, will laugh at us if we renounce the H-bomb. What does anyone imagine they are doing now?

QUESTIONS AND REFERENCES

1. The *Tribune* was a major supporter of CND. Does the argument given here seem to favor unilateral abandonment of nuclear weapons, or does it merely demand negotiation for an international agreement?

2. This article was published three years before the Cuban missile crisis. Look up the historical facts about that event and compare what actually happened with the *Tribune's* predictions.

3. Is the logical conclusion from Joseph Alsop's argument that:
    (1) America should abandon the H-bomb unilaterally?
    (2) money should be diverted into conventional armaments?
    (3) there is no danger of war?
    (4) only countries without a conscience can profit by nuclear threats?

THE LABOUR PARTY CONFERENCE OF 1960

The period between the Labour Party Conference at Brighton in 1957 and that at Scarborough in 1960 was one of increasing polarization of the positions of the radical and conservative wings of the party on the issue of nuclear weapons. Bevan's 1957 speech had disappointed and shocked the radicals; it had also left them confused. It was evident that although few in the party wished to continue the nuclear race, there was fundamental disagreement as to the best way of withdrawing from it. No doubt a few right wingers agreed with Tory leaders that British prestige must be upheld and that this could be accomplished by retaining the bomb. A larger number of party members, but still a minority, agreed with the *Tribune* that it was laughable to suppose that the Russians would be impressed with Britain's tiny nuclear power. The Gallup polls showed that not more than 30 percent of the British public ever favored unilateralism.[4] Although a larger percentage of Labour voters were counted among the unilateralists, it was evident that, as Bevan believed, Labour could never win an election on this issue, and therefore would never be in a position to do anything about nuclear weapons.

At the 1958 Conference the unilateralists were again defeated, and in 1959, because of the election defeat, no conference was held. In 1960, however, it was evident that the unilateralists were prepared to take major action on the nuclear issue. Until 1960 the party structure had operated against them, since the rules permitted labor unions to cast bloc votes on conference issues. (In a giant organization like the Transport and General Workers' Union, a majority of one within the union may be converted into a bloc of a million and a quarter votes for or against an issue—a procedure comparable to the electoral college in an American presidential election.) In most previous conferences the votes of all the big unions had been cast for the "platform," that is, for the side of an issue favored by the executive committee who occupied positions on the platform. In 1960, however, several of the big unions: the Amalgamated Engineers; the National Union of Railwaymen; the Union of Shop, Distributive and Allied Workers; and the huge Transport and General Workers Union, came to Scarborough prepared to support the unilateralist resolution against the wishes of the platform.

The CND was determined to press its advantage. In addition to the votes of the big unions, they had won substantial support in constituency parties. The radicals within and without the party structure sponsored mass rallies and marches to give the impression of solid support of public opinion. At Easter, 1960, a crowd estimated by some to be as high as 50,000 showed their hostility to the bomb by massing in Trafalgar Square at the end of the third annual march from the atomic energy installation at Alder-

[4] Christopher Driver, *The Disarmers* (London: Hodder and Stoughton, Ltd., 1964), p. 99.

maston. In this overheated atmosphere, the Scarborough Conference of 1960 convened.

Debate at Scarborough

FRANK COUSINS VS. HUGH GAITSKELL

The debate over unilateralism at the 1960 Conference may best be characterized as a personal struggle between two men: Frank Cousins, head of the TGWU, and Hugh Gaitskell, leader of the Labour party after the retirement of Clement Attlee. Cousins was the dynamic new left-leaning head of the most powerful union in Britain. In 1957 he had been persuaded by Bevan's speech not to press for a unilateralist resolution, but he had grown increasingly radical since that year, and in 1960 he emerged as the primary spokesman for the unilateralists. Gaitskell, on the other hand, had had no labor union experience. He was an Oxford graduate, an economist, and he had held the posts of Minister of Fuel and Power and of Chancellor of the Exchequer successively in the Attlee governments of 1945–1951. He had been a reformer since his youth and had been associated with the Labour party since the early 1920s. In pre-Conference maneuvering Gaitskell had been instrumental in forming a compromise joint policy statement on the parts of the party executive and the leadership of the Trades Union Congress. This statement pledged that a Labour government would not use the H-bomb first in any conflict, that it would support disengagement in central Europe as a first step in arms control, that Britain would cease trying to be an independent nuclear power, and that although it would not reject the American deterrent, it would, at the same time, try to reduce NATO's reliance on nuclear weapons. In contrast to this, Cousins presented the TGWU resolution, pledging that a Labour government would reject any defense policy based on nuclear weapons, halt their manufacture, and stop flights over Britain by planes carrying nuclear weapons.

The nature of the issues separating the two positions is spelled out in the speeches by Cousins and Gaitskell at the Scarborough Conference. Other speakers echoed the same ideas. The speeches are presented in full from the Report of the Fifty-Ninth Annual Conference of the Labour Party, *1960, pp. 178–180, 195–201. In the vote that followed, the TGWU resolution was approved and the joint policy statement was rejected, both by a narrow margin. As Gaitskell had indicated in his speech, however, he refused to accept the decision of the party, and he succeeded a year later in having the decision reversed.*

Frank Cousins was the sixth speaker in the foreign policy and defense debate. After moving the adoption of the TGWU resolution he spoke as follows:

It is my intention in moving this resolution today to do, if I can, the job that has not been done up to now: that is to explain to you what we are seeking that this Conference should do. I listened to Sam with some great care, and before dealing with our own resolution I should like to answer one or two points he made. I thought he did a magnificent job within the brief he had. So far as he could, he kept it away from personalities, which is to be admired in these very difficult circumstances.[5] I want to say, please Sam, one talks as if those who hold different views are wrecking the show. We in the Transport and General Workers' Union are the ones who asked for a joint meeting with the Labour Party in order that we could formulate a policy which could be accepted by the Party and the trade unions and the elec-

[5] Sam Watson had opened the debate on behalf of the executive committee with a conciliatory and carefully worded appeal for reconsideration of the unilateral resolution. Why does Cousins use the device of speaking directly to Watson when his real target is the Conference delegates?

torate. We asked for that—no one else; and no one, until a recent date, has been too anxious to pursue it.

But when you say to us that there are people with sound and solid views in the Labour Movement who hold this opinion, and that there are others, like Communists and Trotskyists who have jumped on this band wagon, I think you are trying to obscure the issue. Let me say, very proudly, that my organisation stood on this side when the Communists were opposed to us, and if the Communists go on to the other side tomorrow we shall still stand there with our belief that this weapon ought not to be there. And let me say, with great respect to that dear friend of ours personally and of our union, Nye Bevan, that he was the man who said to me: 'Frank, you are wrong. The Russians do not believe that we should polarise this. They think we should retain our weapon.' I do not agree with Mr. Krushchev on this and on a lot of things, but it has nothing to do with the resolution in front of the Labour Party at this moment.

Sam said the British electorate would be the final arbiters. Well, we have been to the country a couple of times,[6] talking along the lines of the policy of the N.E.C.,[7] and the British electorate were the arbiters. Despite everything else we did, they told us they would not have us. I am convinced that had we gone to them with the right policy included in our manifesto, those people, young in mind and young in heart, and many young in age, who marched at Aldermaston would have marched with us in order to get the electors to support us.

Then Sam said we have never had a document which included so much agreement. That is quite true. There is only one simple issue of difference between us on it: the N.E.C. believe that the policies of the Western Alliance and our own country ought to be based on the theory of having the bomb; we think they ought to be based on the opposite

[6] Cousins is referring to electoral defeats in 1955 and 1959, when the party line was much less critical of British foreign and defense policy than it was in 1960, as shown by the resolution of the Executive Committee in that year.

[7] National Executive Committee.

theory of not having the bomb. We think that our defence policy is completely contradictory to the foreign policy of this country. We talk of having friendship with Russia, recognising the compatibility of the two different systems and recognising the two different economic systems—and then threaten them with the bomb.

George Brown[8] has said that we ought to patch up differences. George Brown, over the last few months, has shown more political courage than most people. I disagree with him; but he has said that we are trying to reach an understanding, and believed that we could get out of the use of the bomb at some future date.

There are people who have tried to patch it up, simply on the basis that if we won the vote here that is the end of the problem. But it just is not the end of the problem.

Let me just say to you what we in our resolution have asked for. We have asked that this Conference should recognise that the majority of the people of the country are afraid of the danger of an accidental drift into war. That has obviously occurred because not only has our own leader said it, but so have the leaders of the other political parties. And when you get an issue like that agreed upon by Macmillan and our own leader, and Nye Bevan, obviously that is something that is agreed about.

We ask that our defence policy should be based on the belief that we should not, or should not threaten, to use nuclear weapons. Obviously the Labour Party must agree with that, because they say it in their own document.

We ask for 'the permanent cessation of the manufacture and testing of nuclear and thermonuclear weapons.' They agree to that. In fact, it is part of the Party statement.

But we then ask for something that is not agreed to. We ask that the 'patrols of aircraft carrying nuclear weapons and operating from British bases' should cease forthwith.

I should like to make an interesting point here. Sam, by some slip of his tongue, said that we had based our policy on

8 In 1960 George Brown was deputy leader of the Labour party, second only to Gaitskell.

the defence policy of 1958. I would ask Sam to read that, because that is exactly what we asked the international sub-committee of the joint body that was looking at the document to do. If they had agreed that, we could have been nearer agreement now than ever we have been before in our lives, because the 1958 document says that. It does in fact say that we are opposed to the aircraft carrying missiles over our country. We went on record as saying that the great danger outweighed the advantage. When the first policy document was prepared for acceptance by the joint committee it included that. George Brown will be able to substantiate this when he comes to the rostrum. Out of our honesty of purpose we pointed out to the committee that included in this was a reference to the 1958 policy statement, which meant that we would not have even American bombers floating overhead with nuclear weapons, and because of that it was struck out.

I ask you, who is it that would have difficulty in going back to their constituencies and telling them they had changed their minds?—not those who stood with the policy, but those who changed their minds about the policy.

We have said very clearly, as far as we could, that we want a strengthening of the United Nations Organisation. Everybody agrees on that. And we want them to include China in the deliberations, because everybody realises and recognises that in the system of world affairs, talking about the balance of power and pretending that China is not there, is just nonsense. We in the Labour Movement have said that, so therefore there is no disagreement between us.

What is the disagreement? The disagreement is about Britain's right, by some means or the other, to possess nuclear weapons.[9] I ask you to look carefully at what is being said, because if we have the right to possess the nuclear weapons, then every other country in the world has that same right. And if they have the right, how do we ever get into that atmosphere of avoiding the accidental drift into war?

[9] This is the heart of the argument, as Cousins plainly states it.

Ian Mikardo said—and I thought this ought to be well-recognised by you—that when we are talking about political control over N.A.T.O. we are pretending. There can be no political control over an organisation that has its very activity related to the pressure of buttons which set off missiles. Some of you know that very great pressures are being put on the American Government to insist that we have this kind of pressure.

Some of you will have read yesterday's paper, where it said that 500 of our busmen in one part of the country had said that I had no right to speak for unilateralism. I am sure that you would have read that, because it got some very big headlines.[10] It might also interest you to know that, as recently as Friday, I was talking with my bus committee in London, and they went on record as saying that while they certainly want me to handle their major problems in the bus world, how much more they want me to handle this problem of the bomb, because without solving that the others do not exist.

Our whole policy is based on this fear of Russia. We talk with one breath about the economic threat that comes from that country, and yet we go on paralysing our own economy.

Harold Wilson made a very interesting suggestion on nationalised defence. It would be lovely, nationalising industries that are involved in defence, and, if we got that, half of the problem would go. But we talk as if we can go on spending millions on a useless defence policy and then economically compete with Russia.

I want to remind you that some of the things that are said in the Labour Party policy statement should bear very close examination by you, because Sam talks about our being repudiated if ever we were to tell the electorate in this country that we had surrendered the defence of these fair isles. Of course we would, and we would deserve it. But we are putting out a policy statement that says that we would never use these weapons first, and at the same time having

[10] This charge had not been brought up in the debate. Why did Cousins deal with it? Is he effective in doing so?

to accept that you can never use it second as far as this island is concerned.

I want it to be understood by everyone of you that we regard ourselves as the real patriots in our organisation, who can say to the people that this is an attempt to make you an expendable base for America. You know, they have used this phraseology, and they have talked now of a new theme of survivability in a nuclear war. I think that is inevitable. People in China and America are saying that it must come, and we can measure out the pieces of the world that will escape the holocaust.

Let us add our bit to it. Let us say that if two mad groups in the world want to have a go at each other, we want no part of either of them.

When people say to me, do I think the Western Alliance should have nuclear weapons whilst the Russians have them, I say that I am not talking for the Western Alliance, I am talking for Britain.[11]

When I mentioned to you that you would no doubt have read that little extract from one of the newspapers, which will not get a 'commercial' from me, you no doubt read the other column which did not get such a big headline. It said this: 'N.A.T.O. is the new fourth nuclear power. The American bid to convert N.A.T.O. from a defensive shield into a fourth strategic H-bomb power has already been achieved. The 45 Jupiter rockets now being set up in Italy and Turkey carry the same H-bomb warheads as those in the United States. Both the rockets and the warheads are firmly under the control of United States General Norstadt.' See what it says—that we are going to ally ourselves to a policy where the control of policy is in the hands of the military. The general is undoubtedly a great believer in peace; but he is undoubtedly a greater believer in the sanctity of the American way of life.

The American way of life is probably all right; the Rus-

11 Much of Gaitskell's speech deals with the validity of this question. Which speech deals with it more adequately?

sian way of life is probably all right. But our way of life certainly is all right, and we do not want to jeopardise it.

It is said, and will be said to us later, that N.A.T.O. cannot survive unless we accept nuclear weapons. You realise what that means, that it can never be, apparently, a collective security organisation unless we are prepared to let our territory be the base from which they operate.

When I am asked if it means getting out of N.A.T.O., if the question is posed to me as simply saying, am I prepared to go on remaining in an organisation over which I have no control, but which can destroy us instantly, my answer is Yes, if the choice is that. But it is not that.

Following Cousins' speech nineteen delegates representing a variety of views discussed the issues before the Conference. The twentieth to appear was Hugh Gaitskell, who summed up the position of the platform as follows:

On one thing we can agree. This has been a magnificent debate, argued with passion and conviction and courage on all sides. But I should like to start by trying, despite the television lights, to lower the temperature a little. I want to do that because I think you would wish me before I come to the issues which divide us to recall the things on which we are united. We must remember what lies ahead and not seek to widen the breach that may exist.

We are all agreed on many things in this policy statement. There is not a member of this audience who does not wholly agree that our first principle is support, not only for the United Nations Charter as it is—and if there were any doubts about that they were dispelled at the time of Suez—but for the idea that ultimately only world government can guarantee peace and freedom for humanity.

We are agreed, are we not, on the essential need for all-round, comprehensive, controlled disarmament. I do not think the unilateralists disagree with us on that. They surely must see that the only ultimate solution must come along that road. If they have doubts, I hope they were dispelled by that wonderful, moving speech of Philip Noel-Baker this morning.

There are other things in this document on which I think we do not disagree. If you will put on one side for the moment the N.A.T.O. issue and assume we are still members of N.A.T.O., then I believe we should all agree on the policies which we seek to implement—the policy, for instance, of disengagement in Central Europe which we in the House of Commons have supported for the past $2\frac{1}{2}$ years. I believe that we are agreed that it is impossible to conceive of the disarmament negotiations succeeding unless and until China becomes a party to them. I think we are agreed that there is really no chance of making the United Nations what we should like it to be unless and until the Communist Government of China takes her rightful seat in the United Nations. I think we are all agreed that we passionately want the negotiations on nuclear tests to succeed, not only because this at least will remove the fear of poisoning the atmosphere in the future from such tests but because if they do succeed it will give us the first example of international control over disarmament in the territories of the major nuclear powers of the world. I think we are agreed that we do not intend to resume nuclear tests ourselves.

I think we are agreed, if we remain in N.A.T.O., that there are many changes we should like to see made. We are agreed, for example, that it was wrong and is wrong that Western Germany should have nuclear weapons. We are agreed that the strategy of N.A.T.O. is at present far too strongly based upon the use of nuclear weapons should a conflict of any kind break out. We are agreed that we want to see the emphasis shifted from the early use of nuclear weapons, so that should—which God forbid!—such a conflict arise, then it could be handled by conventional forces, at least for a time, so that a pause can be given before the ghastly possibility of using nuclear weapons arises. We are agreed that we need to establish clearly and firmly that it is not for the generals to decide whether or not the awful decision of using nuclear weapons should be taken. That must be a decision of Governments. We are agreed we want to do everything we can to prevent the spread of nuclear weapons within, as well as outside, the Alliance. We are agreed, as we have said for a long time in the House of Commons, that the Thor missile bases, manned by British troops, should not have been proceeded with. We are agreed on all this and on something else, too.

We are agreed that in the future Britain should not attempt to produce and provide her own effective nuclear weapons.

That is a great deal, you know, on which to agree, and I endorse wholeheartedly what Sam Watson and George Brown said: that we, who have been responsible for working out this policy, could, I think, have hoped, with the give and take which was involved in it—I admit that—that this policy might have been accepted easily by the overwhelming majority of our Party.

What, then, is it on which we disagree? Several speakers have said—and I am glad they have done so—that we do not disagree on whether we want peace. It would be an appalling insult for any member of this Party to say of any other that he wanted war. We do not disagree on whether we want to see the end of the H-bomb and all nuclear weapons, and, indeed, of all armaments everywhere. We do not disagree that ultimately the only solution must be, as I have said, disarmament of national states, and a world government.

What, then, is it on which we disagree? I will discuss a little later on the particular resolutions which are before us but I want first to deal with what I believe to be the issues of principle which have been woven into the whole fabric of the debate. We disagree about what is called unilateral nuclear disarmament.[12]

[12] Here Gaitskell fully accepts the basic issue posed in Cousins' speech. Unilateral abandonment of Britain's nuclear weapon is the only major disagreement.

What does it mean?—unilateral disarmament by Britain. Now you might perhaps conceivably interpret that phrase as meaning no more than the decision in our policy that Britain in future should no longer be an independent nuclear power. There may be some delegates, some members of the Party, who when reading or thinking about or discussing unilateral nuclear disarmament by Britain have thought of it only in those terms. But I do not think that those who most passionately advocate this policy mean only that by unilateral nuclear disarmament. It is certainly not what the Campaign for Nuclear Disarmament means—and I will come to that in a moment.

Our policy, as I have said, is that in the light of the abandonment of Blue Streak by the Tory Government—with all the waste, incidentally, that was involved in trying to start it—Great Britain should give up the idea of being an independent nuclear power in future. Now I do not want any misunderstanding about this. It is easy for Michael Foot to point to me and say, 'There! The Leader of the Party has advocated this idea in the past.' So I have. It was the policy of the Party. And on what grounds did I defend it? On the grounds that I believe to be right, namely, that the possession by Britain of nuclear weapons, as apart from the question of the possession by the West of nuclear weapons, was justified, and indeed could only be justified, because it gave us, as it did, a certain degree of independence—additional independence—from the United States.

But I will say this: I have never taken the view that the decision made originally by the Labour Government in 1945 to manufacture our own atom bomb, or the subsequent decisions which followed, were the kind of things which involved us in a matter of principle. Why, at Scarborough, in this very hall, two years ago I went out of my way to emphasise that because we believed that it was necessary to hold on to our own bombs then, this did not mean that we were going on and on manufacturing nuclear weapons.

As recently as last March, in the Defence debate in the

House of Commons, I explained again the case for this policy. It has been quoted many times in *Tribune*. They do not usually quote the other things I say. They do not usually quote the case that I made at the same time, trying to express a reasonable view of this profoundly difficult issue, the case against our having our own nuclear weapons. I ended that passage of my speech by saying that this was not, in my opinion, a matter of principle but a matter of the balance of arguments, economic, military and technical, on which a cool re-examination and re-appraisal was certainly necessary from time to time.

I am not going to apologise because before the abandonment of Blue Streak I stood by the policy of our own independent weapons; but I accept and wholly agree that, that decision having been taken, it would be ridiculous for us to attempt to produce what in effect will be the only efficient nuclear weapons in future, namely, missiles.

I can give you a number of reasons for that, but I will mention only two. First of all, I think it is economic nonsense for us, when the United States is spending more than the whole of our defence expenditure on research and development into missiles alone, to try to compete with that. I will give you another argument. We are pledged in this statement—and I agree with it wholeheartedly—to try to prevent in every way we can the spread of nuclear weapons among the N.A.T.O. powers; and, obviously, if we want to do that, it is no use our taking action which would lead to the same action being taken by France and perhaps in time by Western Germany.

Now that is our policy. I do not pretend, I repeat, that we reached this decision because we looked on it as a matter of principle. I want no misunderstanding about this. The Campaign for Nuclear Disarmament are right when they say that we looked upon this as a practical issue. But now I say this to those who believe that we should abandon nuclear weapons on principle—I will not say on moral grounds, because I do not believe that there is a monopoly of morality in this matter; if morality comes into it, and if we are to judge on moral grounds we should give the praise to those who advocate the things which will be most likely to achieve peace.

No. But those who advocate unilateral nuclear disarmament by Britain on grounds of principle are bound to ask themselves this question: are they then taking the line—to use Ted Hill's words—that we have nothing to do with nuclear weapons but that nevertheless we remain within N.A.T.O. Alliance which possesses those weapons? Are they going to take the line that all they want to do is to get rid of what they regard as the moral discredit attaching to Britain's having these weapons, while they can get the security they want because America has them?

There is a conclusion you draw from that, and it is a conclusion which recently, to their credit, the Campaign for Nuclear Disarmament has drawn. For they found it necessary, realising the incompatibility of simply saying that there must be British nuclear unilateral disarmament and remaining in the N.A.T.O. Alliance, to go on to put as one of their aims not only the removal of nuclear bases from which H-bombers or missiles might be launched from British territory, but the revision of and, if need be, withdrawal from any alliance, or treaties, which relies on the possession or use of nuclear weapons.

I respect their honesty. But, you know, very few of the leading spokesmen in this debate have gone as far as that. That is not what Frank Cousins said. That is not what the A.E.U. delegate said. That is not even what Michael Foot said, although he is a member of the Executive Committee of the Campaign for Nuclear Disarmament.

Yet the implication is clear enough, is it not, in those words; and they lie behind these resolutions. The implication is that we go to N.A.T.O., to the Western Alliance, and say, 'Give up your nuclear weapons unilaterally, even if the Soviet Union retain theirs; and if you do not, we withdraw from the Alliance.' True, is it not? That is the argument. And now let us deal with it. It is necessary to say these things because it has been cloaked, even in this debate.

All right. So you are proposing that we should tell N.A.T.O., America and the West to do without nuclear weapons. What is going to be the effect of that? Suppose it were accepted. Are we really so simple as to believe that the Soviet Union, whose belief in the ultimate triumph of world communism is continually reiterated by their spokesmen, are not going to use the power you put into their hands if you do unilaterally disarm in this way? Well, all I can say is this: We believe that the West must retain nuclear weapons so long as the Soviet Union has them.

Strangely enough, Mr. Chairman, a most powerful, vivid argument for our point of view was put forward this morning by none other than Ian Mikardo. You will remember his simile, his example, of the two men and one with the pistol, and you will remember what he said was: 'You would never use nuclear weapons because to do so would involve blowing out your own brains.' Yes, that is true—provided the power of the other chap to retaliate exists; but without it, no! If the West has got no power of retaliation there will be no question of Mr. Krushchev bringing down nuclear bombs on Russia, if he decided to start a war. That is the value of deterrence. I believe it. I believe it to be profoundly true that if either America or Russia, either the West or the Soviet bloc, were to abandon their nuclear weapons unilaterally they place themselves at the mercy of the other side. That is a bit of a temptation, you know.

As has recently been said—though I have said it myself some time ago—if the Japanese had had atomic weapons in 1945, do you think that President Truman would have authorised the dropping of the bomb on Hiroshima? There is no doubt about Russia's attitude on this. Mr. Krushchev himself has repeatedly advocated the value of deterrence so far as Russia is concerned. And when you speak of threatening to use nuclear weapons, he is not averse to threatening from time to time. I do not complain. But if this theory applies to Russia, if he believes that the possibility of retaliation deters the United States or the West from attacking the Soviet Union, why should we not apply the theory the other way round? That is the case—the overwhelming case —for the West retaining nuclear weapons so long as the Russians have them.

But if you were to go to the countries in the alliance, in N.A.T.O., and say to them: 'Please give up your nuclear weapons,' we all know quite well that they would refuse to do it. In my view, they would be right so to refuse. Thus the logic of the unilateralists' position is clear. You cannot escape it. If you are a unilateralist on principle, you are driven in to becoming a neutralist; you are driven to becoming one of those who wish us to withdraw from N.A.T.O. I do not know whether the union concerned—the Amalgamated Engineering Union—appreciates this. I am told that in their debate at their national committee great emphasis was laid on the fact, even by the movers of the unilateral resolution, that this did not involve getting out of N.A.T.O. Well, if they are unilateralists in principle, and therefore opposed to us, then either they mean that they will follow the cowardly, hypocritical course of saying: 'We do not want nuclear bombs, but for God's sake, Americans, protect us,' or they are saying that we should get out of N.A.T.O.

Of course, there have been many speeches in the course of this debate which have not made any bones about it—and I welcome the frankness of those people, like Ted Hill, who have spoken, though I am bound to say that his idea of creating a third force out of the Commonwealth is not a very hopeful start. Would Canada come into it? She is a member of N.A.T.O. Do you think Australia and New Zealand would? India wants no alignments. Perhaps Ted had better think out his list of Commonwealth countries that would join with us before we follow his advice. All I can say is that it would not be much of a force.

What is the case against neutralism? What is the case against our withdrawal from N.A.T.O.—our going it alone? It is surely simply this: N.A.T.O. was created because the nations of Western Europe and ourselves and the United States, felt themselves threatened. I think they were right to feel threatened. I think the behaviour of the Soviet Union under Stalin was quite sufficient to justify an attempt at creating a unity in the West. I have not forgotten—because they were some of the worst years through which we lived—the awful period of the 30s. I remember very well the longing we had then for the democracies of the West to stand at the time with the Soviet Union against Hitler Germany. And I say this to you: If you could have created that alliance, if, above all, the United States of America had been in it, I do not believe we should ever have had a Second World War.

Now I think, as I have said on many occasions before, that if this country withdraws from the N.A.T.O. alliance—which is the logic of this resolution, and do not forget it—then two possibilities emerge. It may be that the whole alliance will break up; it may be that the United States may say: 'Well, we have long-range rockets with which to defend ourselves, our own deterrent; and really, with our best friends and allies out of the alliance, with the sort of difficulties'—and they have them, God knows—'with the governments of France and Germany, we wash our hands of Europe.' Do we really want that? I know there are people who say they would like to see the Americans out. They were glad enough to see them in 1942! Of course, the breakup of the alliance will leave the individual countries of Western Europe exposed to any threat or pressure from the Soviet Union.

I know that you can say: 'Well that is all right; Krushchev does not mean any harm.' Let me tell you what I think about Russia's policy. I do not believe that the policy of the Soviet Union is incautious. I do not believe that Mr. Krushchev has any intention of deliberately starting an aggressive war in present circumstances. I do not believe any country has the intention of doing this. But I do believe that if you give them the opportunity of advancing the cause they believe in without cost or serious risk to themselves, they will not reject the opportunity. I ask you, bearing in mind all these things, and reflecting on the events of recent years—

what they did in Hungary, even their attempt to influence affairs in the Congo outside the United Nations—to say that it would not be wise for us to take the risk.

I know some who would say: 'Well, we are, after all, a long way away.' The United Kingdom, if it could be brought within the Soviet orbit by threats, would be a tremendous triumph for Russia. It could be—if we were alone and had nothing to defend ourselves with. You have to think of these things; they are real possibilities in the world as it is today.

I know that there are some people who say: 'But we would rather be overrun by the Soviet Union and become a Communist State than risk war'; and of course there are some people who would like that—we know there are: if not in the floor of this hall, in the galleries today.

I do not want that, and it is not necessary, because I believe that we can have our freedom and peace at the same time so long as we remain loyal to our alliances and to our friends.

What is the other alternative? It has been mentioned, too. It is probably the more likely one, and it is that the alliance goes on without Britain in it. People talk about our having an influence. Even so, do you really think that the Americans, having lost those whom they regarded as their closest friends and allies, would be disposed, in face of what they would regard as a complete betrayal, to listen to us?

There is only one thing that we can say is certain in this —they will have to replace the strength they lose from our withdrawal, and there is no doubt at all about where that will come from: it will come from Western Germany. You have to think of it.

There is another argument. Heaven knows, we have criticised and attacked and prodded the British Government; and, heaven knows, we are not satisfied with the foreign policy that they have pursued. But I think that our efforts in the House of Commons have at least, through the rousing of public opinion at home, made them into the least aggressive of the great Powers in N.A.T.O. I think at least we can say that, because of our efforts, a British Prime Minister did make an attempt, even if it was only the Election that made him do it, to get a Summit meeting.

I do not want to see the influence of Britain removed from the N.A.T.O. alliance. I do not want to see it removed because I believe that this is the best hope we have of building bridges between East and West.

That is our case—the case against unilateralism: therefore, the case against neutralism.

I turn to the resolutions. First, the one on Germany, Resolution No. 24. Now, Mr. Chairman, this resolution contains, of course, opposition to the rearming of Western Germany with nuclear weapons. We are opposed to the rearming of Western Germany with nuclear weapons. So, I am glad to say is the Social Democratic Party of Western Germany. We have fought for this in the House of Commons, and we shall continue to do so. If that was all the resolution contained, there would be no problem. But it contains other things. It refers to what is called the ideology of the Nazi Party. I do not deny—I would be the last person to deny—the dangers of a possible recrudescence of Nazism in Germany. But I think what John Hynd had to say on this subject was justified. Reference has been made to Fritz Erler and to the S.P.D. Fritz Erler spoke to me about this before the debate. He was worried about this resolution. He asked me to see that it was not carried and not accepted, because he said it would do them a great deal of damage in Germany as it stands. I will tell you why—because it goes much further than merely opposing nuclear arms for Germany. It opposes the whole rearming of Western Germany. Yes, I know there are people who opposed that policy a few years ago. Do you really want at this moment to reintroduce that particular subject?

Let me say to Michael Foot that he is quite wrong in supposing that we changed our mind on the rearming of Western Germany. I will not go over the argument. We have always opposed the rearming of Germany with nuclear weapons. Indeed, we do not want to see any nuclear weapons in Central Europe at all. But quite obviously we cannot accept a resolution which says that it opposes the rearming of Western Germany. Nor can I say honestly that it makes good sense to say to the Germans in N.A.T.O. that we will not have a single German soldier over here. You cannot treat your allies like that, and the only effect of doing that is to drive them elsewhere. I do not think it is very likely that there will be many here.

We appreciate that many of those who supported this motion did so, principally at least, having in mind the nuclear rearmament of Western Germany. The seconder of the motion spoke of nothing else. So we ask Conference to remit that particular resolution. I hope that the movers and seconders will agree to do this in a good spirit, for otherwise I have to ask for its rejection. Whatever they are thinking, I think it is right to bear in mind what I have said about our friend Fritz Erler, whose record you heard from Dennis Healey.

Now I turn to the A.E.U. resolution and the T. & G.W.U. resolution. The first thing I say about them is that a great many other resolutions were withdrawn in their favour. We cannot ignore entirely what those other resolutions say. No less than 60 of them were for coming out of N.A.T.O., and I have given you the reasons why we regard that as a disastrous policy. Therefore, I must ask, on behalf of the Executive, that Conference reject Resolution No. 33, the A.E.U. resolution. I agree that there is much in the first four or five lines which is well in line with the policy statement. But if we were to say, in some sense or other, that unilateral renunciation of the testing, manufacture and so on, was to be interpreted only in ths sense that it might have been used, to refer to the policy in the statement, I believe we should be the laughing stock of the country. I do not believe there is the slightest doubt, whatever the A.E.U. may have said, that all the motions behind this were in favour of unilateralism in principle and are, therefore, I think, in favour of neutralism.

I come to the Transport and General Workers' resolution

No. 60. I must confess that I still find it difficult to understand the precise meaning of some of this. We do not disagree with the preamble. Of course not; it is in our document. We do not disagree with the last two clauses. What do we disagree with? We disagree with the implication, as I have made plain, of unilateralism on principle which, perhaps, may be said to run through it.

Let me say this to Frank Cousins. I could not quite understand why he brought in the business about the patrol flights. One of his principal arguments for opposing our document and recommending theirs was that he said our document did not mention the stopping of H-bomb patrols. But it does. It does in the second paragraph, where we re-affirm the policies of the previous years to which he drew attention. He seems to have missed that one. I have sat through all these negotiations, and I can only say I never recollect this particular point being made before. It was not made at the T.U.C. Anyway, it is certainly not a reason, if I may say so, for voting against the policy statement.

Frank Cousins said something else. He said: 'What is the use of advocating friendship with Russia and threatening her with the bomb?' You know, first of all there has been a bit of threatening on the other side. But secondly, to say that is a travesty of the attitude of the Executive towards our relationship with Russia.

I come to the main issue. The main issue is contained, of course, in paragraph (a): 'A complete rejection of any defence policy based on the threat of the use of strategic or tactical nuclear weapons.' Frank Cousins was asked whether that meant only what the policy statement says, namely, that N.A.T.O. should change its strategy and should in future put the emphasis upon conventional rather than nuclear weapons of defence, or whether it means—and it is a fair question in the light of all this great argument—that N.A.T.O. must give up nuclear weapons unilaterally, and whether we must get out of N.A.T.O. I leave it to Conference to decide whether we had a clear answer to those questions. We can only judge. We do not know. But we cannot ignore against the fact that 60 resolutions demanding the withdrawal from N.A.T.O. supported the Transport and General Workers' resolution.

Now the point about it is this. Either the difference between the policy statement and the Transport and General Workers' resolution is a minor one or it is not. If it is almost negligible, as some of my colleagues believe. But if that is the case, how can one explain the determined opposition of the General Secretary of the union to the policy statement? I am sure we can expect a great union of this kind to have regard to the need for unity in the Party, and if there are minor points of difference I cannot see the justification either for the resolution or for the opposition to the policy statement.

Perhaps you will say they are not minor, that they are major differences. All right. I have given you the arguments, and if that is the case, of course we ask for the rejection of the resolution.

There is one other possibility to which I must make reference, because I have read so much about it—that the issue here is not really defence at all but the leadership of this Party. Let me repeat what Manny Shinwell said. The place to decide the leadership of this Party is not here but in the Parliamentary Party. I would not wish for one day to remain a Leader who had lost the confidence of his colleagues in Parliament. It is perfectly reasonable to try to get rid of somebody, to try to get rid of a man you do not agree with, who you think perhaps is not a good Leader. But there are ways of doing this. What would be wrong, in my opinion, and would not be forgiven, is if, in order to get rid of a man, you supported a policy in which you did not wholeheartedly believe, a policy which, as far as the resolution is concerned, is not clear.

Before you take the vote on this momentous occasion, allow me a last word. Frank Cousins has said this is not the end of the problem. I agree with him. It is not the end of the problem because Labour Members of Parliament will have to consider what they do in the House of Commons. What do you expect of them? You know how they voted in June overwhelmingly for the policy statement. It is not in dispute that the vast majority of Labour Members of Parliament are utterly opposed to unilateralism and neutralism. So what do you expect them to do? [13] Change their minds overnight? To go back on the pledges they gave to the people who elected them from their constituencies? And supposing they did do that. Supposing all of us, like well-behaved sheep were to follow the policies of unilateralism and neutralism, what kind of an impression would that make upon the British people? You do not seem to be clear in your minds about it, but I will tell you this. I do not believe that the Labour Members of Parliament are prepared to act as time servers. I do not believe they will do this, and I will tell you why—because they are men of conscience and honour. People of the so-called Right and so-called Centre have every justification for having a conscience, as well as people of the so-called Left. I do not think they will do this because they are honest men, loyal men, steadfast men, experienced men, with a lifetime of service to the Labour Movement.

There are other people too, not in Parliament, in the Party who share our convictions. What sort of people do you think they are? What sort of people do you think we are? Do you think we can simply accept a decision of this kind? Do you think that we can become overnight the pacifists, unilateralists and fellow travellers that other people are? How wrong can you be? As wrong as you are about the attitude of the British people.

In a few minutes the Conference will make its decision. Most of the votes, I know, are predetermined and we have been told what is likely to happen. We know how it comes about. I sometimes think, frankly, that the system we have,

---

[13] Notice the sharp break here with the conciliatory tone of much of the early portion of the speech. Although the audience's attitude is not recorded in the official report, newspaper accounts attest that this portion of Gaitskell's speech evoked a hostile response.

by which great unions decide their policy before even their conferences can consider the Executive recommendation is not really a very wise one or a good one. Perhaps in a calmer moment this situation could be looked at.

I say this to you: we may lose the vote today and the result may deal this Party a grave blow. It may not be possible to prevent it, but I think there are many of us who will not accept that this blow need be mortal, who will not believe that such an end is inevitable. There are some of us, Mr. Chairman, who will fight and fight and fight again to save the Party we love. We will fight and fight again to bring back sanity and honesty and dignity, so that our Party with its great past may retain its glory and its greatness.

It is in that spirit that I ask delegates who are still free to decide how they vote, to support what I believe to be a realistic policy on defence, which yet could so easily have united the great Party of ours, and to reject what I regard as the suicidal path of unilateral disarmament which will leave our country defenceless and alone.

QUESTIONS AND REFERENCES

1. What are the basic premises from which Cousins and Gaitskell are operating? Are they the same ones? Do differences in premises obscure areas of agreement? Would it be possible for the two men to agree? To what extent can each identify with his listeners?

2. Within the context of the speeches, to what degree does each of the speakers make use of existing conditions and events to further his arguments? In rhetorical terms, do they make the best use of the "available means of persuasion"?

3. To what extent does each of the speakers rely on careful reasoning and factual evidence? on loaded language and emotionally charged supporting materials? Do some parts of the speeches contain both elements?

4. How much of the appeal of each speaker is based on his personality, intelligence, character, and reputation? Do they differ in this reliance on "ethical persuasion"? Given the audience situation, whose ethos is greater? Who makes more skillful use of it in the speech?

5. To what extent is each speaker appealing to an audience beyond the Conference—courting party public opinion or that of the general

British public? Would a different emphasis on this aspect have been desirable?

6. For greater perspective on the relationship between the Labour party and the CND, see George Thayer, *The British Political Fringe* (London: Anthony Blond, Ltd., 1965), Chapter 8, and Christopher Driver, *The Disarmers* (London: Hodder and Stoughton, Ltd., 1964).

Five

◗ ◗ ◗

Epilogue

At the very moment of its victory over the platform at Scarborough, the Campaign for Nuclear Disarmament was undergoing a process of internal disintegration. The founding sponsors of the movement had hoped that "CND would make so realistic an intrusion into the political life of the country that it would effectively change British defence and foreign policy, and persuade Britain to rid itself of any dependence upon nuclear power for military purposes." [1] A large portion of the original participants thought that victory had been won at Scarborough, and they were prepared to close the books on the movement. But they failed to take seriously enough either the determination of Hugh Gaitskell to reverse the decision or the problem posed by Lord Russell's organization of the Committee of 100, which was pledged to direct action rather than to political pressure.

The Scarborough vote in all probability did not represent a real majority of the Labour party. Most observers believe that not more than 40 to 45 percent of the members actually

[1] L. John Collins, *Faith Under Fire* (London: Leslie Frewin, Ltd., 1965), p. 326.

favored the unilateral resolution. It was the bloc vote of the big unions that carried the day. But the unilateralists failed to carry on the struggle within the party. Instead of consolidating their position by working actively to win even more converts and secure a second favorable vote in 1961, they diverted effort to sit-down demonstrations and even lost public favor by encouraging confrontations leading to violence in a nonviolent cause.

Meanwhile the party leadership mounted a counterattack through the medium of an organization called the Campaign for Democratic Socialism. Gaitskell and his associates appeared at union conferences and constituency party meetings, winning sufficient adherents so that the narrow unilateralist majority of 1960 was decisively reversed at Blackpool in 1961.

The effect of this reversal was to demoralize what was left of the political wing of the CND. Their plan for capture of the Labour party having been frustrated, they had no alternate plan, and they left the field to the activists. Pressures on the government were no longer in the political arena; they moved into the streets and public squares and to American and British nuclear installations. Mass arrests followed violent confrontations at the close of a Trafalgar Square rally in September of 1961. Attempts to invade and take over nuclear air bases not only were spectacularly unsuccessful, but they brought about prosecutions under the Official Secrets Act of 1911. More important, perhaps, public sympathy for the movement rapidly declined as more and more illegal actions were attempted.

One critic of the movement[2] cites as the campaign's most serious failure an absence of a firm intellectual foundation. Slogans abounded, emotions ran high, but a broad policy capable of uniting diverse groups within clearly defined narrow limits was never achieved. Disillusioned young activists lost sight of their narrow goal and diluted the thrust of their efforts to achieve unilateral disarmament by spread-

[2] George Thayer, *The British Political Fringe* (London: Anthony Blond, Ltd., 1965), p. 175.

ing out to protests against apartheid, neutralism, Vietnam, Biafra, and bacteriological warfare.

Yet it should not be supposed that CND failed to leave its mark on British foreign and defense policies. It seems probable that it hastened, though it did not cause, the adoption of the nuclear test ban. Although Labour party leaders could not endorse unilateralism, CND forced them to take a position hostile to major dependence on nuclear weapons. And although the Labour party in power from 1964–1970 did not abandon nuclear weapons, it has moved toward placing them under international command and exerted its influence in NATO councils to reduce NATO dependence on the deterrent theory.

The CND has maintained a rather precarious existence since Canon Collins left the chairmanship in 1964. It no longer commands the support of nationally known figures. Its records, as we discovered in our search in the summer of 1968, are in total disarray. Yet it may well have contributed, as Canon Collins believes, to "a radical change in the habits of thought which have been implanted in us over centuries." A substantial portion of a new generation sought to replace fighting for country with the attainment of peace as "their duty and glory." [3]

[3] Collins, *op. cit.,* p. 349.